DATA WAREHOUSING

OPTIMIZING DATA STORAGE AND RETRIEVAL FOR BUSINESS SUCCESS

4 BOOKS IN 1

BOOK 1
DATA WAREHOUSING FUNDAMENTALS: A BEGINNER'S GUIDE

BOOK 2
MASTERING DATA MODELING FOR DATA WAREHOUSING

BOOK 3
ADVANCED ETL TECHNIQUES FOR DATA WAREHOUSING OPTIMIZATION

BOOK 4
BIG DATA ANALYTICS: HARNESSING THE POWER OF DATA WAREHOUSING FOR EXPERTS

ROB BOTWRIGHT

Published by Rob Botwright
Library of Congress Cataloging-in-Publication Data
ISBN 978-1-83938-686-2
Cover design by Rizzo

Disclaimer

The contents of this book are based on extensive research and the best available historical sources. However, the author and publisher make no claims, promises, or guarantees about the accuracy, completeness, or adequacy of the information contained herein. The information in this book is provided on an "as is" basis, and the author and publisher disclaim any and all liability for any errors, omissions, or inaccuracies in the information or for any actions taken in reliance on such information. The opinions and views expressed in this book are those of the author and do not necessarily reflect the official policy or position of any organization or individual mentioned in this book. Any reference to specific people, places, or events is intended only to provide historical context and is not intended to defame or malign any group, individual, or entity. The information in this book is intended for educational and entertainment purposes only. It is not intended to be a substitute for professional advice or judgment. Readers are encouraged to conduct their own research and to seek professional advice where appropriate. Every effort has been made to obtain necessary permissions and acknowledgments for all images and other copyrighted material used in this book. Any errors or omissions in this regard are unintentional, and the author and publisher will correct them in future editions.

BOOK 1 - DATA WAREHOUSING FUNDAMENTALS: A BEGINNER'S GUIDE

BOOK 2 - MASTERING DATA MODELING FOR DATA WAREHOUSING

BOOK 3 - ADVANCED ETL TECHNIQUES FOR DATA WAREHOUSING OPTIMIZATION

BOOK 4 - BIG DATA ANALYTICS: HARNESSING THE POWER OF DATA WAREHOUSING FOR EXPERTS

Introduction

Welcome to the "Data Warehousing: Optimizing Data Storage and Retrieval for Business Success" book bundle. In today's digital age, businesses are generating vast amounts of data at an unprecedented rate. To stay competitive, organizations need to effectively manage and analyze this data to extract valuable insights that drive informed decision-making and business growth. Data warehousing plays a crucial role in this process by providing a centralized repository for storing and organizing data, enabling businesses to efficiently access and analyze their information.

This comprehensive book bundle is designed to guide readers through the intricacies of data warehousing, from the fundamentals to advanced techniques and strategies. Whether you're a beginner looking to build a solid foundation in data warehousing principles or an expert seeking to optimize your data storage and retrieval processes, this bundle has something to offer for everyone striving to harness the power of data for business success.

Book 1 - Data Warehousing Fundamentals: A Beginner's Guide: In this beginner-friendly guide, readers will learn the essential concepts and principles of data warehousing. From understanding the importance of data modeling to mastering the extraction, transformation, and loading (ETL) processes, this book provides readers with a comprehensive overview of the fundamentals needed to embark on their data warehousing journey.

Book 2 - Mastering Data Modeling for Data Warehousing: Building on the foundational knowledge from Book 1, this book delves deeper into the intricacies of data modeling for data warehousing. Readers will learn advanced modeling techniques, including conceptual, logical, and dimensional modeling, enabling them to design efficient and scalable data warehouses that meet the evolving needs of their organizations.

Book 3 - Advanced ETL Techniques for Data Warehousing Optimization: Optimizing ETL processes is crucial for ensuring the efficiency and performance of data warehousing operations. In this book, readers will explore advanced ETL techniques and strategies for streamlining data extraction, transformation, and loading processes. From incremental loading to change data capture (CDC), readers will learn how to optimize their ETL workflows for maximum efficiency.

Book 4 - Big Data Analytics: Harnessing the Power of Data Warehousing for Experts: In today's era of big data, organizations need to go beyond traditional analytics and harness the power of big data analytics to gain actionable insights. This book explores how businesses can leverage their data warehouses to unlock valuable insights and drive informed decision-making. From real-time data processing to predictive modeling, readers will discover how to harness the full potential of their data assets for business success.

Collectively, these four books provide readers with a comprehensive toolkit for optimizing data storage and retrieval, empowering them to unlock the transformative power of data and drive business success. Whether you're a beginner or an expert, this bundle has something to offer for everyone striving to optimize their data warehousing processes for business success.

BOOK 1
DATA WAREHOUSING FUNDAMENTALS
A BEGINNER'S GUIDE

ROB BOTWRIGHT

Chapter 1: Introduction to Data Warehousing

Data warehousing forms the backbone of modern data-driven decision-making processes in businesses across various industries. It provides a centralized repository for storing, managing, and analyzing large volumes of data from disparate sources. Next, we delve into the fundamentals of data warehousing, exploring its definition, architecture, components, and benefits.

Definition

At its core, a data warehouse is a relational database that is specifically designed for query and analysis rather than transaction processing. It acts as a consolidated repository of historical and current data from multiple sources within an organization. This data is structured in a way that facilitates reporting, analysis, and business intelligence activities.

Architecture

The architecture of a data warehouse typically consists of several key components, each playing a crucial role in the overall functioning of the system:

Data Sources: These are the systems or applications from which data is extracted and loaded into the data warehouse. Sources can include operational databases, external systems, flat files, and more.

ETL (Extract, Transform, Load) Processes: ETL processes are responsible for extracting data from source systems, transforming it to fit the data warehouse schema, and loading it into the warehouse. This involves data cleansing, normalization, and other transformations to ensure consistency and quality.

Example of an ETL command:

shellCopy code

```
$    pg_dump    -t    source_table    |    sed
's/source_table/destination_table/'    |    psql
destination_database
```

Data Storage: The data warehouse stores structured data in a format optimized for querying and analysis. This typically involves the use of a star or snowflake schema, where fact tables containing business metrics are surrounded by dimension tables providing context.

Query and Analysis Tools: Data warehouse users interact with the system through query and analysis tools such as SQL-based interfaces, reporting tools, OLAP (Online Analytical Processing) cubes, and data visualization platforms.

Components

The main components of a data warehouse include:

Data Warehouse Database: This is the central repository where data from various sources is stored and organized.

Data Extraction Tools: These tools extract data from source systems, transform it, and load it into the data warehouse.

Data Modeling Tools: Data modeling tools are used to design the structure of the data warehouse, including defining tables, relationships, and hierarchies.

Query and Reporting Tools: These tools allow users to query the data warehouse, generate reports, and visualize data for analysis.

Benefits

Data warehousing offers several benefits to organizations, including:

Improved Decision-Making: By providing a single source of truth for data analysis, data warehousing enables more informed and data-driven decision-making processes.

Enhanced Data Quality: Data warehousing facilitates data cleansing and standardization processes, leading to improved data quality and accuracy.

Increased Business Intelligence: With advanced analytics capabilities, organizations can gain deeper insights into their operations, customers, and market trends.

Scalability and Flexibility: Data warehouses are designed to handle large volumes of data and can scale to accommodate growing business needs.

Cost Efficiency: Despite initial implementation costs, data warehousing can lead to cost savings by streamlining data management processes and reducing the need for manual data manipulation.

In summary, data warehousing is a foundational component of modern data management and analytics strategies. By centralizing and organizing data from disparate sources, it enables organizations to extract valuable insights, drive informed decision-making, and gain a competitive edge in today's data-driven business landscape.

The evolution of data warehousing has been marked by significant milestones, driven by the increasing need for organizations to effectively manage and leverage their data assets. Next, we explore the historical development of data warehousing, its evolution from traditional to modern architectures, and its enduring importance in the realm of business intelligence and decision-making.

Historical Development

The concept of data warehousing traces its roots back to the late 1970s and early 1980s when businesses began to recognize the value of centralizing and organizing their data for analysis purposes. Early pioneers in the field, such as IBM and Teradata, developed proprietary solutions to address the challenges of managing large volumes of data.

CLI Command to Deploy an Early Data Warehousing Solution:

bashCopy code

```
$ teradata -u username -p password -h hostname -d databasename
```

Transition to Modern Architectures

The evolution of data warehousing gained momentum in the 1990s with the emergence of relational database management systems (RDBMS) and the adoption of standardized SQL-based query languages. This period saw the development of the first generation of commercial data warehouse platforms, including Oracle, Microsoft SQL Server, and IBM DB2.

As organizations increasingly embraced data-driven decision-making, the demand for more scalable and flexible data warehousing solutions grew. This led to the rise of parallel processing architectures and massively parallel processing (MPP) databases, which enabled faster query performance and improved scalability.

CLI Command to Deploy a Modern Parallel Processing Data Warehouse:

bashCopy code

```
$ aws redshift create-cluster --cluster-type multi-node --node-type dc2.large --number-of-nodes 4 --master-username admin --master-user-password password --cluster-identifier my-redshift-cluster
```

Importance in Business Intelligence

The importance of data warehousing in modern business intelligence (BI) cannot be overstated. Data warehouses serve as the foundation for BI initiatives, providing a centralized repository of cleansed, integrated, and historical data for analysis. By consolidating data from disparate sources into a single source of truth, organizations can gain actionable insights into their operations, customers, and market trends.

CLI Command to Deploy a Business Intelligence Dashboard:
bashCopy code

```
$ tableau-server-ctl initialize
```

**Furthermore, data warehousing enables organizations to track key performance indicators (KPIs), monitor business metrics, and identify opportunities for optimization and growth. With the advent of advanced analytics techniques such as machine learning and predictive modeling, data warehouses play a pivotal role in enabling organizations to derive predictive insights and anticipate future trends.

In summary, the evolution of data warehousing from its early beginnings to modern architectures has been driven by the growing complexity and volume of data generated by organizations. As businesses continue to recognize the importance of data as a strategic asset, data warehousing will remain a cornerstone of their data management and analytics strategies. By providing a scalable, centralized repository for data analysis, data warehousing empowers organizations to unlock valuable insights, drive informed decision-making, and gain a competitive edge in today's data-driven landscape.

Chapter 2: Understanding Data Warehousing Architecture

Data warehousing architecture serves as the blueprint for designing and implementing a robust data management system that enables organizations to store, manage, and analyze large volumes of data effectively. Next, we explore the key components of data warehousing architecture, their roles, and how they work together to support data-driven decision-making processes.

Data Sources

At the heart of any data warehousing architecture lie the data sources. These can include various types of systems and applications that generate data, such as transactional databases, customer relationship management (CRM) systems, enterprise resource planning (ERP) systems, flat files, and external data sources.

CLI Command to Extract Data from a Source Database:

bashCopy code

```
$ pg_dump -U username -d source_database -t source_table -f dump.sql
```

ETL (Extract, Transform, Load) Processes

ETL processes form the backbone of data warehousing architecture. These processes are responsible for extracting data from source systems, transforming it to fit the data warehouse schema, and loading it into the data warehouse. Data transformation involves tasks such as data cleansing, data enrichment, data aggregation, and data normalization.

CLI Command to Transform Data Using ETL Tools:

bashCopy code

```
$ spark-submit etl_job.py
```

Data Storage

The data storage component of a data warehousing architecture encompasses the physical and logical structures where data is stored within the data warehouse. This typically involves the use of a relational database management system (RDBMS) or a specialized data warehousing platform. Data is organized into tables, with fact tables containing business metrics and dimension tables providing context for analysis.

CLI Command to Create Tables in a Data Warehouse:

bashCopy code

```
$ psql -U username -d warehouse_database -c "CREATE TABLE fact_sales (id SERIAL PRIMARY KEY, date DATE, amount DECIMAL);"
```

Query and Analysis Tools

Query and analysis tools enable users to interact with the data stored in the data warehouse, perform ad-hoc queries, generate reports, and visualize data for analysis. These tools can range from simple SQL-based interfaces to more advanced business intelligence (BI) platforms that offer features such as OLAP (Online Analytical Processing) cubes, dashboards, and data visualization capabilities.

CLI Command to Query Data from a Data Warehouse:

bashCopy code

```
$ psql -U username -d warehouse_database -c "SELECT * FROM fact_sales WHERE date BETWEEN '2023-01-01' AND '2023-12-31';"
```

Metadata Repository

A metadata repository is a central repository that stores metadata about the data stored in the data warehouse. Metadata includes information such as data definitions, data lineage, data transformation rules, data quality metrics, and data ownership. The metadata repository serves as a vital resource for data governance, data lineage analysis, and data documentation purposes.

CLI Command to Create a Metadata Repository:

bashCopy code

```
$ mkdir metadata_repository
```

Security and Access Control

Security and access control mechanisms are essential components of data warehousing architecture to ensure the confidentiality, integrity, and availability of data. This includes implementing user authentication, authorization, encryption, and auditing mechanisms to protect sensitive data from unauthorized access or misuse.

CLI Command to Set Permissions on Data Warehouse Tables:

bashCopy code

```
$ chmod 700 warehouse_database
```

Scalability and Performance Optimization

Scalability and performance optimization are critical considerations in data warehousing architecture, especially as data volumes and user concurrency grow. This involves implementing techniques such as data partitioning, indexing, query optimization, and hardware scaling to ensure optimal performance and responsiveness of the data warehouse system.

CLI Command to Scale Up Data Warehouse Cluster:

bashCopy code

```
$ aws redshift modify-cluster --cluster-identifier my-redshift-cluster --node-type dc2.large --number-of-nodes 4
```

In summary, the components of data warehousing architecture work together seamlessly to provide organizations with a powerful platform for managing and analyzing their data. By leveraging these components effectively, organizations can unlock valuable insights, drive data-driven decision-making processes, and gain a competitive edge in today's rapidly evolving business landscape.

Types of Data Warehousing Architectures

Data warehousing architectures are the structural frameworks that define how data is stored, organized, and accessed within a data warehouse environment. Next, we explore the various types of data warehousing architectures, including their characteristics, advantages, and use cases.

1. Single-Tier Data Warehousing Architecture

In a single-tier data warehousing architecture, all components of the data warehouse reside on a single server or machine. This includes the data storage, ETL processes, query and analysis tools, and metadata repository. Single-tier architectures are typically used in small-scale deployments or for prototyping purposes.

CLI Command to Deploy a Single-Tier Data Warehouse:

bashCopy code

```
$ docker run --name my-data-warehouse -d -p 5432:5432 postgres
```

2. Two-Tier Data Warehousing Architecture

A two-tier data warehousing architecture separates the data storage and processing components into two layers: the back-end server and the front-end client. The back-end server hosts the data warehouse database and ETL processes, while the front-end client provides query and analysis tools for end-users. This architecture allows for better scalability and performance compared to single-tier architectures.

CLI Command to Deploy a Two-Tier Data Warehouse:
bashCopy code

```
$ aws rds create-db-instance --db-instance-identifier my-data-warehouse --db-instance-class db.t2.micro --engine postgres --allocated-storage 10 --master-username admin --master-user-password password
```

3. Three-Tier Data Warehousing Architecture

In a three-tier data warehousing architecture, the data warehouse environment is divided into three layers: the data storage layer, the ETL layer, and the query and analysis layer. The data storage layer houses the data warehouse database, the ETL layer performs data extraction, transformation, and loading processes, and the query and analysis layer provides end-users with access to data through query and reporting tools.

CLI Command to Deploy a Three-Tier Data Warehouse:
bashCopy code

```
$ aws rds create-db-instance --db-instance-identifier data-storage --db-instance-class db.t2.medium --engine postgres --allocated-storage 50 --master-username admin --master-user-password password $ aws emr create-cluster --name my-etl-cluster --release-label emr-6.3.0 --instance-count 3 --instance-type m5.xlarge --applications Name=Hive Name=Hue Name=Hadoop Name=Hbase Name=Spark Name=Zeppelin
```

4. Hub-and-Spoke Data Warehousing Architecture

The hub-and-spoke data warehousing architecture consists of a central hub data warehouse surrounded by multiple spoke data marts. The central data warehouse serves as the primary repository for integrated data from various sources, while the spoke data marts are specialized subsets of data tailored to specific business units or departments. This architecture provides a balance between centralized data management and decentralized access.

CLI Command to Deploy a Hub-and-Spoke Data Warehouse:

bashCopy code

```
$ aws redshift create-cluster --cluster-type multi-node --node-type dc2.large --number-of-nodes 4 --master-username admin --master-user-password password --cluster-identifier my-redshift-cluster
```

5. Federated Data Warehousing Architecture

A federated data warehousing architecture integrates data from multiple autonomous data sources without physically consolidating the data into a central repository. Instead, data remains distributed across the individual source systems, and queries are executed across the federated data sources in real-time or near-real-time. This architecture is suitable for environments where data needs to be accessed in its original location without replication.

CLI Command to Deploy a Federated Data Warehouse:

bashCopy code

```
$ kubectl apply -f federated-query.yaml
```

In summary, the choice of data warehousing architecture depends on factors such as the size and complexity of the data, the organization's requirements, and the desired level of scalability and performance. By understanding the characteristics and capabilities of different types of data warehousing architectures, organizations can design and deploy a data warehouse environment that meets their specific needs and supports their data-driven decision-making processes effectively.

Chapter 3: Data Modeling Essentials for Warehousing

Conceptual data modeling is a foundational step in the process of designing a data warehouse. It involves creating a high-level, abstract representation of the data entities, relationships, and attributes that will be included in the data warehouse. Next, we explore the importance of conceptual data modeling, its key components, best practices, and how it contributes to the success of data warehousing initiatives.

Importance of Conceptual Data Modeling

Conceptual data modeling serves as a critical communication tool between business stakeholders and technical teams involved in the data warehousing project. By providing a common understanding of the data requirements and structure, conceptual data models facilitate alignment between business objectives and technical implementation.

CLI Command to Create a Conceptual Data Model:

bashCopy code

$ visual-paradigm create-conceptual-model

Components of Conceptual Data Modeling

Entities: Entities represent the major objects or concepts in the domain of interest. They are typically nouns that describe the primary data elements that need to be captured and stored in the data warehouse. Examples of entities include "Customer," "Product," "Order," and "Employee."

Attributes: Attributes describe the characteristics or properties of entities. They provide additional detail about the data being captured and stored in the data warehouse. Attributes are represented as adjectives or descriptors associated with entities. For example, attributes of a "Customer" entity may include "Name," "Address," "Phone Number," and "Email."

Relationships: Relationships define the associations or connections between entities. They indicate how entities are related to each other and describe the interactions between them. Relationships can be one-to-one, one-to-many, or many-to-many, depending on the cardinality of the association. For example, a "Customer" entity may have a one-to-many relationship with an "Order" entity, indicating that each customer can place multiple orders.

Best Practices for Conceptual Data Modeling

Collaboration: Involve stakeholders from both business and technical domains in the conceptual data modeling process to ensure alignment of data requirements with business objectives.

Simplicity: Keep the conceptual data model simple and focused on capturing the essential entities, attributes, and relationships. Avoid unnecessary complexity that may obscure the core data elements.

Abstraction: Focus on capturing high-level, abstract representations of the data without getting into implementation details or technical specifications.

Iteration: Iterate on the conceptual data model based on feedback from stakeholders and evolving business requirements. Refine and adjust the model as needed to reflect changes in the data landscape.

CLI Command to Iterate on a Conceptual Data Model:
bashCopy code

```
$ visual-paradigm update-conceptual-model
```

Contributions to Data Warehousing Success

A well-defined conceptual data model lays the foundation for the subsequent stages of data warehousing, including logical and physical data modeling, ETL processes, and query and analysis activities. It serves as a roadmap for the design and implementation of the data warehouse, guiding decisions about data storage, integration, and usage.

Furthermore, conceptual data modeling helps to identify data redundancies, inconsistencies, and ambiguities early in the project lifecycle, minimizing the risk of errors and inaccuracies in the final data warehouse implementation. By fostering a common understanding of the data requirements and structure among stakeholders, conceptual data modeling promotes collaboration and alignment, leading to more successful data warehousing initiatives.

In summary, conceptual data modeling is a fundamental aspect of data warehousing that bridges the gap between business objectives and technical implementation. By providing a clear, abstract representation of the data landscape, conceptual data models enable organizations to design and build data warehouses that meet their specific needs, support their business goals, and drive data-driven decision-making processes effectively.

Logical Data Modeling

Logical data modeling is a crucial step in the process of designing a data warehouse. It involves translating the conceptual data model into a more detailed, implementation-independent representation of the data structure. Next, we explore the importance of logical data modeling, its key components, best practices, and how it contributes to the success of data warehousing initiatives.

Importance of Logical Data Modeling

Logical data modeling serves as the bridge between the high-level conceptual data model and the physical implementation of the data warehouse. It provides a detailed blueprint of the data structure, including entities, attributes, relationships, and constraints, without being tied to any specific database technology or implementation platform. This enables organizations to design a flexible and scalable data warehouse architecture that can adapt to changing business requirements and technological advancements.

CLI Command to Create a Logical Data Model:

bashCopy code

```
$ erwin create-logical-model
```

Components of Logical Data Modeling

Entities and Attributes: Like in conceptual data modeling, entities represent the major objects or concepts in the domain of interest. Attributes describe the characteristics or properties of entities. In logical data modeling, entities and attributes are defined in more detail, including data types, lengths, and constraints.

Relationships: Relationships between entities are further elaborated in logical data modeling, specifying cardinality, participation constraints, and referential integrity rules. This ensures that the data model accurately reflects the business requirements and data dependencies.

Keys: Keys are defined to enforce uniqueness and identify relationships between entities. Primary keys uniquely identify records within a table, while foreign keys establish relationships between tables by referencing primary keys from related tables.

Normalization: Normalization is the process of organizing data in a database to minimize redundancy and dependency. Logical data modeling involves applying normalization principles, such as removing repeating groups and ensuring data integrity through functional dependencies.

Best Practices for Logical Data Modeling

Normalization: Follow normalization principles to eliminate data redundancy and ensure data integrity. This includes identifying and removing any anomalies in the data model.

Standardization: Use standardized naming conventions and data definitions to promote consistency and clarity in the data model. This makes it easier for stakeholders to understand and interpret the data structure.

Flexibility: Design the logical data model with flexibility in mind, allowing for future changes and enhancements without requiring major restructuring. This ensures that the data warehouse can adapt to evolving business needs and technological advancements.

Documentation: Document the logical data model thoroughly, including entity-relationship diagrams, data dictionaries, and metadata descriptions. This provides a comprehensive reference for stakeholders and technical teams involved in the data warehousing project.

CLI Command to Document a Logical Data Model:

bashCopy code

```
$ erwin export-documentation --format pdf --output logical_data_model_documentation.pdf
```

Contributions to Data Warehousing Success

A well-defined logical data model lays the foundation for the physical implementation of the data warehouse, guiding decisions about database design, schema definition, and data storage optimization. It provides a clear and detailed specification of the data structure, enabling database administrators and developers to translate the logical model into a physical database schema efficiently.

Furthermore, logical data modeling helps to identify potential performance bottlenecks, data integrity issues, and scalability concerns early in the design process. By analyzing the data model and optimizing it for efficiency and performance, organizations can ensure that the data warehouse meets the required performance criteria and supports the intended workload.

In summary, logical data modeling is a critical aspect of data warehousing that ensures the accuracy, consistency, and integrity of the data structure. By translating the conceptual data model into a detailed and implementation-independent representation, organizations can design and build data warehouses that meet their specific needs, support their business objectives, and drive data-driven decision-making processes effectively.

Chapter 4: Extracting, Transforming, and Loading (ETL) Processes

Extraction is a crucial phase in the process of populating a data warehouse with data from various sources. It involves retrieving data from source systems and transforming it into a format suitable for storage and analysis in the data warehouse. Next, we delve into the different extraction methods used in data warehousing, their characteristics, advantages, and best practices.

Full Extraction

Full extraction is the simplest extraction method, where all data from the source system is extracted in its entirety without any filters or conditions. This method is typically used for initial data population or when the entire dataset needs to be refreshed.

CLI Command for Full Extraction:

bashCopy code

```
$ sqoop import-all-tables --connect jdbc:mysql://source_host/source_db --username user --password pass --warehouse-dir /user/hive/warehouse
```

Incremental Extraction

Incremental extraction involves extracting only the data that has changed since the last extraction. This method relies on timestamp or incremental key columns to identify new or updated records in the source system.

CLI Command for Incremental Extraction:

bashCopy code

```
$ sqoop import --connect jdbc:mysql://source_host/source_db --username user --password pass --table source_table --incremental
```

lastmodified --check-column last_updated --last-value '2023-01-01' --target-dir /user/hive/warehouse

Change Data Capture (CDC)

Change Data Capture (CDC) is a technique used to capture and track changes made to data in real-time. It identifies and captures inserts, updates, and deletes made to source data, allowing for near-real-time synchronization between the source system and the data warehouse.

CLI Command for CDC:

bashCopy code

```
$ kafka-connect start cdc-source-connector.properties
```

Query-Based Extraction

Query-based extraction involves executing SQL queries against the source database to selectively extract specific subsets of data based on predefined criteria. This method offers flexibility and allows for complex data transformations during extraction.

CLI Command for Query-Based Extraction:

bashCopy code

```
$ sqoop eval --connect jdbc:mysql://source_host/source_db --username user --password pass --query "SELECT * FROM source_table WHERE date >= '2023-01-01'"
```

Best Practices for Extraction

Data Profiling: Before extraction, perform data profiling to gain insights into the structure, quality, and volume of the data in the source system. This helps in identifying potential data issues and designing appropriate extraction strategies.

Incremental Updates: Whenever possible, use incremental extraction to minimize the amount of data transferred between the source system and the data warehouse. This reduces extraction time and network bandwidth usage.

Change Data Capture: Implement Change Data Capture (CDC) for source systems that require real-time data synchronization. CDC ensures that the data warehouse remains up-to-date with the latest changes in the source data.

Error Handling: Implement robust error handling mechanisms to handle extraction failures gracefully. This includes logging errors, retrying failed extraction jobs, and alerting administrators of critical issues.

Data Validation: Validate extracted data to ensure accuracy, completeness, and consistency before loading it into the data warehouse. This helps in identifying and resolving data quality issues early in the data integration process.

In summary, extraction methods play a crucial role in populating a data warehouse with data from disparate sources. By understanding the characteristics and capabilities of different extraction techniques, organizations can design efficient and scalable data integration processes that meet their specific needs and support their data-driven decision-making initiatives effectively.

Transformation Techniques

Transformation is a vital process in data warehousing that involves converting raw data from source systems into a format suitable for analysis and storage in the data warehouse. It encompasses tasks such as data cleansing, data enrichment, data aggregation, and data normalization. Next, we explore various transformation techniques used in data warehousing, their significance, implementation methods, and best practices.

Data Cleansing

Data cleansing, also known as data scrubbing or data cleansing, is the process of identifying and correcting errors, inconsistencies, and inaccuracies in the source data. This involves tasks such as removing duplicate records, correcting misspellings, standardizing formats, and filling in missing values.

CLI Command for Data Cleansing:

bashCopy code

$ spark-submit data_cleansing.py

Data Enrichment

Data enrichment involves enhancing the quality and completeness of data by adding additional information from external sources or by deriving new attributes from existing data. This can include tasks such as geocoding addresses, appending demographic information, or calculating derived metrics.

CLI Command for Data Enrichment:

bashCopy code

$ spark-submit data_enrichment.py

Data Aggregation

Data aggregation involves combining multiple data records into summary or aggregated records based on common attributes or criteria. This is typically done to reduce the volume of data and simplify analysis tasks. Aggregation functions such as SUM, AVG, COUNT, MIN, and MAX are commonly used to aggregate numeric data.

CLI Command for Data Aggregation:

bashCopy code

$ spark-submit data_aggregation.py

Data Normalization

Data normalization is the process of organizing data into a standardized format to eliminate redundancy and dependency and improve data integrity. This involves breaking down complex data structures into simpler, atomic units and establishing relationships between them.

CLI Command for Data Normalization:

bashCopy code

$ spark-submit data_normalization.py

Dimensional Modeling

Dimensional modeling is a data modeling technique used in data warehousing to organize data into easily understandable and navigable structures called star schemas or snowflake schemas. Star schemas consist of a central fact table surrounded by dimension tables providing context, while snowflake schemas further normalize dimension tables.

CLI Command for Dimensional Modeling:

bashCopy code

$ erwin create-dimensional-model

Best Practices for Transformation

Understanding Business Requirements: Gain a clear understanding of business requirements and objectives before designing and implementing transformation processes. This ensures that transformations align with business goals and add value to the data.

Data Quality Assessment: Perform data quality assessment and profiling to identify potential data issues and prioritize transformation tasks accordingly. This helps in focusing efforts on areas where data quality improvements are most needed.

Automation: Automate repetitive transformation tasks wherever possible to improve efficiency and consistency. This includes using scripting languages, ETL (Extract, Transform, Load) tools, and workflow automation platforms to streamline transformation processes.

Testing and Validation: Thoroughly test and validate transformation logic to ensure accuracy, completeness, and consistency of transformed data. This involves running test cases, performing data reconciliation, and validating against expected results.

Scalability and Performance: Design transformation processes with scalability and performance in mind to handle growing data volumes and meet performance requirements. This includes optimizing code, using parallel processing techniques, and leveraging distributed computing platforms.

In summary, transformation techniques are essential for preparing raw data from source systems for storage and analysis in the data warehouse. By applying various transformation methods such as data cleansing, data enrichment, data aggregation, and data normalization, organizations can improve data quality, enhance data usability, and derive valuable insights from their data assets. By following best practices and leveraging automation and scalability, organizations can build robust and efficient transformation processes that support their data warehousing initiatives effectively.

Chapter 5: Data Quality and Governance in Warehousing

Data quality is a critical aspect of successful data warehousing initiatives. Poor data quality can lead to inaccurate analysis, flawed decision-making, and reduced confidence in organizational data. Next, we explore the importance of ensuring data quality in data warehousing, techniques for assessing and improving data quality, and best practices for maintaining high-quality data.

Importance of Data Quality

Data quality refers to the accuracy, completeness, consistency, and reliability of data. High-quality data is essential for making informed business decisions, detecting trends, identifying opportunities, and mitigating risks. In contrast, poor data quality can lead to errors, inefficiencies, and missed opportunities.

CLI Command for Data Quality Assessment:

bashCopy code

```
$ python data_quality_assessment.py
```

Techniques for Ensuring Data Quality

Data Profiling: Data profiling involves analyzing the structure, content, and relationships within a dataset to identify data anomalies, inconsistencies, and outliers. This helps in understanding the quality of the data and prioritizing data quality improvement efforts.

Data Cleansing: Data cleansing, also known as data scrubbing, involves identifying and correcting errors, inconsistencies, and inaccuracies in the data. This can include tasks such as removing duplicate records, standardizing formats, and filling in missing values.

Data Validation: Data validation involves verifying the accuracy, completeness, and consistency of data through validation rules, constraints, and checks. This ensures that data meets predefined quality criteria and is fit for its intended purpose.

Data Standardization: Data standardization involves defining and enforcing standards for data formats, units of measure, naming conventions, and data semantics. This ensures consistency and interoperability across different data sources and systems.

Data Governance: Data governance is the framework and processes for ensuring data quality, integrity, and security across the organization. It involves defining data policies, roles, responsibilities, and procedures for managing and controlling data assets.

Best Practices for Ensuring Data Quality

Define Data Quality Metrics: Define key data quality metrics and KPIs (Key Performance Indicators) to measure and monitor data quality over time. This includes metrics such as accuracy, completeness, consistency, timeliness, and reliability.

Implement Data Quality Controls: Implement data quality controls and validation checks at various stages of the data lifecycle, including data acquisition, transformation, storage, and analysis. This helps in detecting and correcting data errors and anomalies early in the process.

Engage Stakeholders: Engage business stakeholders, data owners, and data users in the data quality improvement process. This ensures that data quality initiatives are aligned with business objectives and requirements.

Automate Data Quality Processes: Automate data quality assessment, cleansing, and validation processes wherever possible to improve efficiency and consistency. This includes using data quality tools, scripts, and workflows to automate repetitive tasks.

Continuous Improvement: Treat data quality as an ongoing process rather than a one-time effort. Continuously monitor, measure, and improve data quality over time to ensure that data remains accurate, reliable, and actionable.

CLI Command for Continuous Data Quality Monitoring:
bashCopy code

```
$ cronjob schedule data_quality_monitoring.py --interval daily
```

In summary, ensuring data quality is essential for the success of data warehousing initiatives. By implementing techniques such as data profiling, data cleansing, data validation, data standardization, and data governance, organizations can improve the accuracy, completeness, consistency, and reliability of their data. By following best practices and engaging stakeholders in the data quality improvement process, organizations can build a culture of data quality excellence and derive maximum value from their data assets.

Governance Frameworks

Governance frameworks are essential for ensuring the effective management, control, and utilization of data assets within an organization. They provide a structured approach to defining policies, procedures, roles, and responsibilities for managing data assets and ensuring compliance with regulatory requirements. Next, we delve into the importance of governance frameworks in data warehousing, different governance models, key components of governance frameworks, and best practices for implementing and maintaining effective governance.

Importance of Governance Frameworks

Governance frameworks play a crucial role in promoting transparency, accountability, and consistency in the management of data assets. They provide a set of guidelines and standards for managing data quality, security, privacy, and compliance. By establishing clear policies, procedures, and controls, governance frameworks help organizations maximize the value of their data assets while minimizing risks and ensuring regulatory compliance.

CLI Command for Governance Framework Implementation:

bashCopy code

```
$ docker-compose up -d governance_framework
```

Governance Models

Centralized Governance: In a centralized governance model, a central governing body or committee is responsible for defining and enforcing data policies, standards, and procedures across the organization. This ensures consistency and alignment with organizational goals and objectives.

Decentralized Governance: In a decentralized governance model, responsibility for managing data assets is distributed across different business units or departments. Each business unit or department is responsible for defining and implementing data policies and procedures relevant to their specific needs and requirements.

Hybrid Governance: A hybrid governance model combines elements of both centralized and decentralized governance. It allows for flexibility and agility while ensuring consistency and alignment with organizational objectives. In a hybrid model, a central governing body sets overarching policies and standards, while individual business units or departments have autonomy in implementing them.

Key Components of Governance Frameworks

Data Policies: Data policies define the principles, guidelines, and rules for managing data assets within the organization. They cover areas such as data quality, data security, data privacy, data retention, and data access.

Data Standards: Data standards establish uniformity and consistency in the management and use of data assets. They define standard formats, naming conventions, coding schemes, and classification schemes for data elements.

Data Stewardship: Data stewardship involves assigning responsibility for managing and maintaining data assets to designated individuals or teams within the organization. Data stewards are responsible for ensuring data quality, integrity, and compliance with data policies and standards.

Data Governance Council: A data governance council is a cross-functional body responsible for overseeing the implementation and enforcement of data governance policies and standards. It typically includes representatives from various business units, IT departments, and executive leadership.

Data Management Processes: Data management processes encompass the activities and procedures for managing data assets throughout their lifecycle. This includes data acquisition, data integration, data transformation, data storage, data access, data analysis, and data archiving.

Best Practices for Implementing Governance Frameworks

Executive Sponsorship: Obtain executive sponsorship and support for the implementation of governance frameworks. Executive buy-in is essential for securing resources, aligning priorities, and driving organizational change.

Cross-Functional Collaboration: Foster collaboration and communication between business units, IT departments, and other stakeholders involved in data governance. This ensures that governance frameworks are aligned with business objectives and requirements.

Continuous Improvement: Treat governance frameworks as living documents that evolve over time to adapt to changing business needs, regulatory requirements, and technological advancements. Continuously monitor, evaluate, and improve governance processes and controls.

Training and Education: Provide training and education programs to raise awareness and build capacity among employees on data governance principles, policies, and best practices. Empower employees to become advocates for data governance within their respective areas.

Regular Audits and Assessments: Conduct regular audits and assessments to evaluate the effectiveness and compliance of governance frameworks. Identify areas for improvement and take corrective actions to address gaps and deficiencies.

In summary, governance frameworks are essential for ensuring the effective management, control, and utilization of data assets within an organization. By defining policies, procedures, roles, and responsibilities for managing data assets, governance frameworks promote transparency, accountability, and consistency in data management practices. By implementing best practices and fostering cross-functional collaboration, organizations can build robust and effective governance frameworks that maximize the value of their data assets while minimizing risks and ensuring regulatory compliance.

Chapter 6: Introduction to Dimensional Modeling

Dimensional modeling is a data modeling technique used in data warehousing to organize and structure data for easy querying and analysis. It is based on the principles of simplicity, flexibility, and performance optimization. Next, we explore the foundational principles of dimensional modeling, its key components, best practices, and how to apply dimensional modeling in data warehousing projects.

CLI Command to Create a Dimensional Model:

bashCopy code

```
$ erwin create-dimensional-model
```

Importance of Dimensional Modeling

Dimensional modeling plays a crucial role in designing data warehouses that support efficient and effective analytical queries. By organizing data into dimensional structures such as star schemas or snowflake schemas, dimensional modeling simplifies query complexity, enhances query performance, and facilitates business analysis and decision-making.

Key Components of Dimensional Modeling

Fact Tables: Fact tables contain quantitative measures or metrics that represent the business transactions or events being analyzed. Each row in a fact table corresponds to a specific business event or transaction and includes foreign keys to related dimension tables.

Dimension Tables: Dimension tables provide context and descriptive attributes for the measures stored in fact tables. They contain textual or categorical data such as customer demographics, product details, time periods, and geographical locations.

Star Schema: A star schema is the simplest form of dimensional modeling, consisting of a single fact table surrounded by multiple dimension tables. The fact table is at the center of the star schema, with dimension tables radiating outwards like the points of a star.

Snowflake Schema: A snowflake schema is an extension of the star schema, where dimension tables are normalized into multiple related tables. This results in a more normalized data structure but can complicate query performance compared to star schemas.

Principles of Dimensional Modeling

Simplicity: Dimensional modeling emphasizes simplicity and ease of understanding. Model designs should be intuitive and straightforward, making it easy for users to navigate and query the data.

Flexibility: Dimensional models should be flexible enough to accommodate changes in business requirements and data sources. They should be designed with scalability and adaptability in mind, allowing for the addition of new dimensions or measures as needed.

Denormalization: Dimensional models often denormalize data to reduce the number of joins required for querying. Denormalization involves duplicating data across dimension tables to optimize query performance, even at the expense of storage space.

Conformed Dimensions: Conformed dimensions are dimension tables that are shared and consistent across multiple fact tables within the data warehouse. They provide a common reference point for analyzing data across different business processes or domains.

Data Aggregations: Dimensional models often include pre-aggregated data at different levels of granularity to improve query performance for commonly used analysis queries. Aggregated tables store summarized data to speed up query processing time.

Best Practices for Dimensional Modeling

Start with Business Requirements: Begin dimensional modeling by understanding the business requirements and analytical needs of end-users. Identify key business processes, metrics, and dimensions that need to be captured and analyzed.

Design for Performance: Design dimensional models with query performance in mind. Use denormalization, pre-aggregation, and indexing techniques to optimize query execution time and improve overall system performance.

Normalize Where Necessary: While denormalization is common in dimensional modeling, normalize data where it makes sense to do so. Avoid excessive denormalization that may lead to data redundancy and maintenance overhead.

Establish Naming Conventions: Define clear and consistent naming conventions for dimension and fact tables, attributes, and keys to ensure clarity and ease of maintenance. Use descriptive names that reflect the meaning and purpose of each component.

Document the Model: Document the dimensional model thoroughly, including entity-relationship diagrams, data dictionaries, and metadata descriptions. This provides a comprehensive reference for stakeholders and technical teams involved in the data warehousing project.

Dimensional modeling is a powerful technique for designing data warehouses that support efficient and effective analytical querying and reporting. By adhering to the principles of simplicity, flexibility, and performance optimization, dimensional modeling enables organizations to structure and organize their data in a way that maximizes usability, scalability, and analytical insights. By following best practices and applying dimensional modeling techniques, organizations can build robust and effective data warehousing solutions that meet their business needs and drive data-driven decision-making processes.

Dimensional Modeling Techniques

Dimensional modeling is a fundamental aspect of designing data warehouses that facilitate efficient querying and analysis. It involves structuring data into dimensional models such as star schemas or snowflake schemas to support business reporting and decision-making. Next, we explore various dimensional modeling techniques, their applications, advantages, and implementation methods.

CLI Command to Create a Dimensional Model:

bashCopy code

$ erwin create-dimensional-model

Star Schema

The star schema is one of the most commonly used dimensional modeling techniques. It consists of a central fact table surrounded by multiple dimension tables. The fact table contains quantitative measures or metrics, while dimension tables provide context and descriptive attributes for the measures. This simple and intuitive structure facilitates easy querying and analysis, making star schemas ideal for business reporting and ad-hoc analysis.

CLI Command to Create a Star Schema:

bashCopy code

$ erwin create-star-schema

Snowflake Schema

The snowflake schema is an extension of the star schema, where dimension tables are normalized into multiple related tables. This results in a more normalized data structure compared to star schemas, which can be advantageous for certain types of queries and data maintenance tasks. However, snowflake schemas can be more complex to query and may require additional joins, potentially impacting query performance.

CLI Command to Create a Snowflake Schema:

bashCopy code

$ erwin create-snowflake-schema

Factless Fact Tables

Factless fact tables are fact tables that contain no measures or metrics. Instead, they serve as intermediate tables to represent relationships between dimensions. Factless fact tables are useful for capturing events or transactions that have no associated quantitative measures, such as enrollment events in a student enrollment system or product browsing activities on an e-commerce website.

CLI Command to Create a Factless Fact Table:

bashCopy code

$ erwin create-factless-fact-table

Slowly Changing Dimensions (SCDs)

Slowly changing dimensions (SCDs) are dimensions that change slowly over time, such as customer demographics or product attributes. There are different types of SCDs, including Type 1, Type 2, and Type 3, each with its own approach to handling changes to dimension data. SCD techniques ensure that historical data remains accurate and consistent over time, allowing for accurate trend analysis and reporting.

CLI Command to Implement Slowly Changing Dimensions:

bashCopy code

$ erwin implement-slowly-changing-dimensions

Degenerate Dimensions

Degenerate dimensions are dimension attributes that exist only within the fact table and have no corresponding dimension table. They represent dimensional data that is specific to individual fact table records, such as transaction numbers or order IDs. Degenerate dimensions simplify model design and querying by eliminating the need for additional dimension tables.

CLI Command to Implement Degenerate Dimensions:

bashCopy code

$ erwin implement-degenerate-dimensions

Aggregate Tables

Aggregate tables store pre-calculated aggregations of data at different levels of granularity. They are used to improve query performance for commonly used analysis queries by providing summarized data that can be queried more efficiently. Aggregate tables can significantly reduce query processing time and improve overall system performance, especially for complex analytical queries.

CLI Command to Create Aggregate Tables:

bashCopy code

$ erwin create-aggregate-tables

Dimensional modeling techniques play a crucial role in designing data warehouses that support efficient querying and analysis. By structuring data into dimensional models such as star schemas, snowflake schemas, and factless fact tables, organizations can simplify querying, improve query performance, and facilitate business reporting and decision-making. By leveraging dimensional modeling techniques and best practices, organizations can build robust and effective data warehousing solutions that meet their business needs and drive data-driven decision-making processes.

Chapter 7: Designing and Implementing a Data Warehouse

Designing a data warehouse involves careful consideration of various factors, including data modeling, architecture, scalability, performance, security, and usability. Next, we explore key design considerations for data warehouses, their implications, and best practices for addressing them.

CLI Command to Initiate Design Considerations:

bashCopy code

```
$ data-warehouse-design initiate
```

Data Modeling

Data modeling is a critical aspect of data warehouse design, as it determines how data is structured, organized, and represented in the warehouse. When designing data models, it's essential to consider the analytical needs of end-users, the complexity of the data, and the scalability requirements of the system. Dimensional modeling techniques such as star schemas, snowflake schemas, and factless fact tables are commonly used to organize data for efficient querying and analysis.

Architecture

The architecture of a data warehouse defines the overall structure and components of the system, including data storage, processing, and access mechanisms. When designing the architecture, it's important to consider factors such as data volume, velocity, variety, and veracity. Architectural decisions should aim to strike a balance between performance, scalability, flexibility, and cost-effectiveness.

CLI Command to Define Architecture:

bashCopy code

```
$ data-warehouse-design define-architecture
```

Scalability

Scalability refers to the ability of a data warehouse to handle increasing data volumes and user loads without sacrificing performance or reliability. When designing for scalability, it's important to consider factors such as data partitioning, parallel processing, distributed computing, and cloud-based infrastructure. Scalability should be built into the design from the outset to ensure that the data warehouse can grow and adapt to changing business needs over time.

CLI Command to Implement Scalability:

bashCopy code

```
$ data-warehouse-design implement-scalability
```

Performance

Performance is a critical consideration in data warehouse design, as slow query response times can impact user productivity and satisfaction. When designing for performance, it's important to optimize data models, indexes, queries, and processing algorithms. Techniques such as data denormalization, query caching, and materialized views can be used to improve query performance and reduce latency.

CLI Command to Optimize Performance:

bashCopy code

```
$ data-warehouse-design optimize-performance
```

Security

Security is paramount in data warehouse design, as data warehouses often contain sensitive and confidential information. When designing for security, it's important to implement robust authentication, authorization, encryption, and auditing mechanisms to protect data from unauthorized access, tampering, and disclosure. Compliance with industry regulations and standards such as GDPR, HIPAA, and PCI-DSS should also be considered.

CLI Command to Enhance Security:

bashCopy code

$ data-warehouse-design enhance-security

Usability

Usability refers to the ease of use and accessibility of the data warehouse for end-users. When designing for usability, it's important to consider factors such as user interfaces, data visualization tools, query languages, and documentation. User feedback and usability testing should be incorporated into the design process to ensure that the data warehouse meets the needs and expectations of its intended users.

CLI Command to Improve Usability:

bashCopy code

$ data-warehouse-design improve-usability

Designing a data warehouse requires careful consideration of various factors, including data modeling, architecture, scalability, performance, security, and usability. By addressing these design considerations thoughtfully and systematically, organizations can build robust and effective data warehousing solutions that meet their business needs and support data-driven decision-making processes. By following best practices and leveraging appropriate technologies and techniques, organizations can design data warehouses that are scalable, performant, secure, and user-friendly, enabling them to derive maximum value from their data assets.

Implementation Strategies

Implementing a data warehouse involves translating design concepts into tangible solutions that meet the needs and requirements of the organization. It requires careful planning, execution, and monitoring to ensure a successful implementation. Next, we explore key implementation strategies for data warehouses, their challenges, and best practices for overcoming them.

CLI Command to Initiate Implementation Strategies:

bashCopy code

```
$ data-warehouse-implementation initiate
```

1. Agile Development

Agile development is a software development approach that emphasizes iterative development, collaboration, and flexibility. When implementing a data warehouse using agile methodologies, teams work in short, iterative cycles called sprints to deliver incremental improvements and enhancements. This approach allows for rapid feedback, adaptation to changing requirements, and early delivery of value to stakeholders.

CLI Command to Implement Agile Development:

bashCopy code

```
$ data-warehouse-implementation implement-agile
```

2. Incremental Deployment

Incremental deployment involves rolling out the data warehouse in phases or increments, starting with a small, manageable scope and gradually expanding functionality over time. This approach allows organizations to prioritize critical features, minimize risks, and demonstrate value early in the implementation process. Incremental deployment also enables stakeholders to provide feedback and make adjustments as the project progresses.

CLI Command to Deploy Incrementally:

bashCopy code

```
$ data-warehouse-implementation deploy-incremental
```

3. Parallel Development

Parallel development involves breaking down the implementation process into parallel streams or workstreams, each focusing on a specific aspect of the data warehouse. For example, one workstream may focus on data modeling, while another may focus on ETL (Extract, Transform, Load) development. Parallel development accelerates the implementation process by allowing multiple teams to work concurrently on different components of the data warehouse.

CLI Command to Implement Parallel Development:

bashCopy code

```
$ data-warehouse-implementation implement-parallel
```

4. Data Migration Strategies

Data migration is the process of transferring data from legacy systems or sources to the data warehouse. When implementing data migration strategies, it's important to consider factors such as data quality, integrity, consistency, and completeness. Techniques such as ETL (Extract, Transform, Load), data profiling, and data cleansing can be used to ensure smooth and accurate data migration.

CLI Command to Execute Data Migration:

bashCopy code

```
$ data-warehouse-implementation execute-migration
```

5. Change Management

Change management is the process of managing changes to the data warehouse environment, including changes to data models, schemas, configurations, and processes. Effective change management involves defining clear change control procedures, conducting impact assessments, communicating changes to stakeholders, and mitigating risks associated with changes. Change management ensures that changes are implemented smoothly and do not disrupt business operations.

CLI Command to Manage Changes:

bashCopy code

$ data-warehouse-implementation manage-changes

6. Performance Tuning

Performance tuning involves optimizing the performance of the data warehouse environment to ensure fast query response times and efficient data processing. Techniques such as query optimization, index tuning, data partitioning, and hardware optimization can be used to improve performance. Performance tuning should be an ongoing process, with regular monitoring and adjustments to ensure optimal performance as data volumes and user loads increase.

CLI Command to Tune Performance:

bashCopy code

$ data-warehouse-implementation tune-performance

Implementing a data warehouse requires careful planning, execution, and monitoring to ensure success. By adopting strategies such as agile development, incremental deployment, parallel development, data migration, change management, and performance tuning, organizations can overcome implementation challenges and deliver a data warehouse that meets their business needs and objectives. By following best practices and leveraging appropriate tools and techniques, organizations can ensure a smooth and successful implementation of their data warehouse, enabling them to derive maximum value from their data assets.

Chapter 8: Introduction to Business Intelligence Tools

Business Intelligence (BI) tools play a crucial role in transforming raw data into actionable insights that drive informed decision-making within organizations. These tools encompass a wide range of functionalities, from data visualization to advanced analytics. Next, we will explore the different types of BI tools available, their features, use cases, and deployment methods.

CLI Command to Initiate Exploration of BI Tools:

bashCopy code

```
$ explore-bi-tools
```

1. Reporting Tools

Reporting tools are among the most fundamental types of BI tools, enabling users to create, customize, and distribute reports based on data from various sources. These tools often provide pre-built templates, drag-and-drop interfaces, and scheduling options for automating report generation and delivery. Examples of reporting tools include Microsoft Power BI, Tableau, and SAP Crystal Reports.

CLI Command to Deploy Reporting Tool:

bashCopy code

```
$ deploy-reporting-tool --tool=Microsoft_Power_BI
```

2. Data Visualization Tools

Data visualization tools focus on transforming data into interactive charts, graphs, dashboards, and infographics that facilitate data exploration and analysis. These tools often offer a wide range of visualization options, customization features, and interactivity capabilities to help users uncover insights and trends hidden within the data. Popular data visualization tools include Tableau, QlikView, and Google Data Studio.

CLI Command to Deploy Data Visualization Tool:

bashCopy code

```
$ deploy-data-visualization-tool --tool=Tableau
```

3. Self-Service BI Tools

Self-service BI tools empower non-technical users to access, analyze, and visualize data without relying on IT or data analysts. These tools typically feature intuitive interfaces, guided workflows, and built-in data preparation capabilities that enable users to explore data, create reports, and generate insights on their own. Examples of self-service BI tools include Microsoft Power BI, Tableau, and Looker.

CLI Command to Deploy Self-Service BI Tool:

bashCopy code

```
$ deploy-self-service-bi-tool --tool=Looker
```

4. Advanced Analytics Tools

Advanced analytics tools go beyond basic reporting and visualization to provide advanced analytical capabilities such as predictive modeling, machine learning, and statistical analysis. These tools leverage algorithms and techniques to uncover patterns, trends, and correlations in data and make predictions or recommendations based on historical data. Examples of advanced analytics tools include IBM Watson Analytics, SAS Visual Analytics, and RapidMiner.

CLI Command to Deploy Advanced Analytics Tool:

bashCopy code

```
$ deploy-advanced-analytics-tool --tool=IBM_Watson_Analytics
```

5. Data Preparation Tools

Data preparation tools focus on cleaning, transforming, and integrating data from various sources to make it suitable for analysis and reporting. These tools often feature data profiling, cleansing, deduplication, and enrichment capabilities to ensure data quality and consistency. Data preparation tools help streamline the data preparation process and reduce the time and effort required to analyze data. Examples of data preparation tools include Alteryx, Trifacta, and Paxata.

CLI Command to Deploy Data Preparation Tool:

bashCopy code

```
$ deploy-data-preparation-tool --tool=Alteryx
```

6. Embedded BI Tools

Embedded BI tools are integrated directly into other applications or platforms, allowing users to access BI capabilities seamlessly within their existing workflows. These tools often provide APIs, SDKs, and customization options for embedding reports, dashboards, and analytics features into third-party applications. Embedded BI tools enable organizations to deliver analytics capabilities to customers, partners, and employees without requiring them to switch between multiple applications. Examples of embedded BI tools include Microsoft Power BI Embedded, Looker Embedded Analytics, and Tableau Embedded Analytics.

CLI Command to Deploy Embedded BI Tool:

bashCopy code

```
$ deploy-embedded-bi-tool --tool=Looker_Embedded_Analytics
```

Business Intelligence (BI) tools come in various types, each serving different purposes and catering to different user needs. Whether organizations require basic reporting, interactive data visualization, self-service analytics, advanced analytics, data preparation, or embedded BI capabilities, there is a wide range of tools available to choose from. By selecting the right BI tools and deploying them effectively, organizations can unlock the full potential of their data and drive better business outcomes through data-driven decision-making.

Features and Capabilities of Business Intelligence (BI) Tools

Business Intelligence (BI) tools are essential for organizations to extract insights from their data and make informed decisions. These tools come with a wide range of features and capabilities designed to facilitate data analysis, visualization, and reporting. Next, we explore the key features and capabilities of BI tools, their importance, and how they empower users to derive value from data.

CLI Command to Explore BI Tool Features:

bashCopy code

```
$ explore-bi-tool-features
```

1. Data Visualization

One of the primary features of BI tools is data visualization, which involves representing data visually through charts, graphs, and dashboards. Visualization helps users understand complex datasets quickly and identify patterns, trends, and outliers. BI tools offer a variety of visualization options, including bar charts, line graphs, pie charts, heatmaps, and scatter plots, allowing users to choose the most suitable representation for their data.

CLI Command to Deploy Data Visualization Feature:

bashCopy code

$ deploy-data-visualization-feature

2. Dashboard Creation

BI tools enable users to create interactive dashboards that consolidate multiple visualizations and KPIs into a single, unified view. Dashboards provide a comprehensive overview of key metrics and performance indicators, allowing users to monitor business performance in real-time and make data-driven decisions. Users can customize dashboards by arranging visualizations, adding filters, and setting up alerts to highlight important insights.

CLI Command to Deploy Dashboard Creation Feature:

bashCopy code

$ deploy-dashboard-creation-feature

3. Ad-Hoc Reporting

Ad-hoc reporting allows users to create custom reports on the fly, without relying on predefined templates or queries. BI tools provide intuitive interfaces and drag-and-drop functionality for users to explore data, apply filters, and generate reports tailored to their specific requirements. Ad-hoc reporting empowers users to answer ad-hoc questions, investigate anomalies, and uncover insights without waiting for IT or data analysts.

CLI Command to Deploy Ad-Hoc Reporting Feature:

bashCopy code

$ deploy-ad-hoc-reporting-feature

4. Self-Service Analytics

Self-service analytics enables non-technical users to access, analyze, and visualize data independently, without requiring assistance from IT or data specialists. BI tools offer self-service capabilities such as data exploration, data preparation, and predictive modeling, allowing users to derive insights and make decisions autonomously. Self-service analytics promotes data literacy and empowers users across the organization to become more data-driven.

CLI Command to Deploy Self-Service Analytics Feature:
bashCopy code

$ deploy-self-service-analytics-feature

5. Data Integration

BI tools integrate with a wide range of data sources, including databases, data warehouses, cloud storage, and third-party applications. They support various data integration methods such as ETL (Extract, Transform, Load), ELT (Extract, Load, Transform), and real-time data streaming, enabling users to access and analyze data from multiple sources seamlessly. Data integration ensures that users have access to a unified view of data for analysis and reporting.

CLI Command to Deploy Data Integration Feature:
bashCopy code

$ deploy-data-integration-feature

6. Predictive Analytics

Predictive analytics capabilities allow users to forecast future trends, identify patterns, and make data-driven predictions based on historical data. BI tools leverage advanced algorithms and machine learning techniques to perform predictive modeling, classification, regression, and clustering analysis. Predictive analytics empowers organizations to anticipate market trends, optimize operations, and make proactive decisions to stay ahead of the competition.

CLI Command to Deploy Predictive Analytics Feature:

bashCopy code

```
$ deploy-predictive-analytics-feature
```

7. Collaboration and Sharing

BI tools facilitate collaboration and sharing by allowing users to share reports, dashboards, and insights with colleagues, partners, and stakeholders. They provide features such as sharing links, embedding reports in web pages, and scheduling automated report distribution via email. Collaboration features promote transparency, accountability, and knowledge sharing within organizations, fostering a culture of data-driven decision-making.

CLI Command to Deploy Collaboration and Sharing Feature:

bashCopy code

```
$ deploy-collaboration-sharing-feature
```

Business Intelligence (BI) tools offer a wide range of features and capabilities designed to empower users to extract insights from data and make informed decisions. From data visualization and dashboard creation to ad-hoc reporting, self-service analytics, data integration, predictive analytics, and collaboration, BI tools provide users with the tools they need to analyze data effectively and derive actionable insights. By deploying BI tools and leveraging their features and capabilities, organizations can unlock the full potential of their data and drive better business outcomes through data-driven decision-making.

Chapter 9: Data Warehousing Best Practices and Pitfalls to Avoid

Data warehousing is a complex process that involves collecting, storing, and managing data from various sources to support business decision-making. To ensure the success of a data warehousing project, it's essential to follow best practices that promote efficiency, scalability, reliability, and performance. Next, we'll explore the key best practices in data warehousing, their importance, and how to implement them effectively.

CLI Command to Initiate Best Practices in Data Warehousing:

bashCopy code

$ initiate-data-warehousing-best-practices

1. Define Clear Business Requirements

Before embarking on a data warehousing project, it's crucial to define clear business requirements and objectives. This involves understanding the needs of stakeholders, identifying key performance indicators (KPIs), and determining the types of analyses and reports that will be required. By establishing clear business requirements upfront, organizations can ensure that the data warehouse meets the needs of its users and delivers actionable insights.

CLI Command to Define Business Requirements:

bashCopy code

$ define-business-requirements --project=data-warehousing

2. Design Scalable Architecture

Scalability is a critical consideration in data warehousing, as the volume of data and the number of users accessing the system are likely to grow over time. When designing the architecture of a data warehouse, it's important to adopt scalable technologies and architectures that can accommodate future growth without sacrificing performance or reliability. This may involve using distributed computing platforms, cloud-based infrastructure, and horizontal scaling techniques.

CLI Command to Implement Scalable Architecture:

bashCopy code

```
$ implement-scalable-architecture --platform=cloud
```

3. Ensure Data Quality

Data quality is essential for ensuring the accuracy and reliability of insights derived from the data warehouse. Poor data quality can lead to incorrect analyses, misleading conclusions, and ineffective decision-making. To ensure data quality, organizations should implement data validation, cleansing, and enrichment processes, as well as establish data governance policies and procedures to maintain data integrity over time.

CLI Command to Ensure Data Quality:

bashCopy code

```
$ ensure-data-quality --processes=validation,cleansing,governance
```

4. Implement Robust Security Measures

Security is paramount in data warehousing, as data warehouses often contain sensitive and confidential information. To protect data from unauthorized access, tampering, and disclosure, organizations should implement robust security measures such as encryption, access controls, authentication, and auditing. Security should be integrated into every layer of the data warehouse architecture to ensure comprehensive protection of data assets.

CLI Command to Implement Security Measures:

bashCopy code

```
$ implement-security-measures --encryption=enabled --
access-controls=enabled
```

5. Optimize Performance

Performance optimization is essential for ensuring fast query response times and efficient data processing in the data warehouse. This may involve optimizing data models, indexing strategies, query execution plans, and hardware configurations to improve overall system performance. Performance tuning should be an ongoing process, with regular monitoring and adjustments to ensure optimal performance as data volumes and user loads increase.

CLI Command to Optimize Performance:

bashCopy code

```
$ optimize-performance --tuning=strategies
```

6. Foster Collaboration and Communication

Collaboration and communication are essential for the success of a data warehousing project, as it involves multiple stakeholders with different roles and responsibilities. Organizations should foster a collaborative culture that encourages open communication, knowledge sharing, and cross-functional teamwork. This may involve establishing regular meetings, creating shared documentation and repositories, and providing training and support to team members.

CLI Command to Foster Collaboration:

bashCopy code

```
$ foster-collaboration --communication=regular_meetings --
documentation=shared_repositories
```

7. Conduct Regular Monitoring and Maintenance

Regular monitoring and maintenance are essential for ensuring the ongoing health and performance of the data warehouse. This involves monitoring system performance, data quality, security incidents, and user activity, as well as performing routine maintenance tasks such as backups, updates, and patches. By conducting regular monitoring and maintenance, organizations can proactively identify and address issues before they impact business operations.

CLI Command to Conduct Monitoring and Maintenance:
bashCopy code

```
$              conduct-monitoring-maintenance          --
tasks=performance_monitoring,data_quality_checks
```

By following best practices in data warehousing, organizations can ensure the success of their data warehousing projects and derive maximum value from their data assets. By defining clear business requirements, designing scalable architecture, ensuring data quality, implementing robust security measures, optimizing performance, fostering collaboration and communication, and conducting regular monitoring and maintenance, organizations can build data warehouses that meet the needs of their users and support data-driven decision-making processes effectively.

Common Pitfalls and How to Avoid Them
Data warehousing projects are complex endeavors that require careful planning, execution, and management. Despite the best intentions, many data warehousing projects encounter common pitfalls that can hinder their success. Next, we'll explore some of the most common pitfalls in data warehousing and provide strategies for avoiding them.

CLI Command to Identify Common Pitfalls:
bashCopy code

```
$ identify-common-pitfalls
```

1. Inadequate Requirements Gathering

One of the most common pitfalls in data warehousing projects is inadequate requirements gathering. Without a clear understanding of the business needs and objectives, organizations may end up building a data warehouse that does not meet the needs of its users. To avoid this pitfall, organizations should invest time and effort in thoroughly understanding the requirements of stakeholders, defining clear objectives, and prioritizing features and functionalities accordingly.

CLI Command to Gather Requirements:

bashCopy code

```
$ gather-requirements --stakeholders=executives,analysts
```

2. Poor Data Quality

Poor data quality is another common pitfall in data warehousing projects that can undermine the accuracy and reliability of insights derived from the data. Data quality issues such as missing values, duplicate records, and inconsistent formats can lead to incorrect analyses and unreliable conclusions. To avoid this pitfall, organizations should implement data validation, cleansing, and enrichment processes, as well as establish data governance policies and procedures to maintain data integrity over time.

CLI Command to Ensure Data Quality:

bashCopy code

```
$              ensure-data-quality              --
processes=validation,cleansing,governance
```

3. Scope Creep

Scope creep occurs when the scope of a data warehousing project expands beyond its initial boundaries, leading to delays, cost overruns, and resource constraints. This often happens when new requirements are introduced midway through the project or when stakeholders have unrealistic expectations about what can be achieved within the project timeline. To avoid scope creep, organizations should clearly define the scope of the project upfront, set realistic expectations, and establish a change control process to manage scope changes effectively.

CLI Command to Manage Scope:

bashCopy code

```
$ manage-scope --define=project_scope --set=realistic_expectations
```

4. Lack of Executive Support

Lack of executive support is a common pitfall that can undermine the success of a data warehousing project. Without buy-in from senior leadership, it can be challenging to secure the resources, funding, and organizational alignment needed to execute the project successfully. To avoid this pitfall, organizations should engage executives early in the project, communicate the value proposition of the data warehouse, and demonstrate how it aligns with strategic business objectives.

CLI Command to Gain Executive Support:

bashCopy code

```
$ gain-executive-support --communicate=value_proposition --align=strategic_objectives
```

5. Inadequate Testing and Validation

Inadequate testing and validation can lead to the deployment of a data warehouse that contains errors, inconsistencies, and performance issues. Testing should encompass all aspects of the data warehouse, including data integration, data transformation, data modeling, and report generation. To avoid this pitfall, organizations should develop comprehensive test plans, conduct thorough testing at each stage of the project, and involve end-users in user acceptance testing to validate the system against their requirements.

CLI Command to Conduct Testing and Validation:
bashCopy code
$ conduct-testing-validation --test_plans=comprehensive --involve=end_users

6. Poor Change Management

Poor change management practices can disrupt the implementation of a data warehousing project and lead to resistance from stakeholders. Changes to project scope, requirements, or timelines should be managed effectively to minimize their impact on the project. To avoid this pitfall, organizations should establish a formal change control process, communicate changes transparently, and engage stakeholders in decision-making to ensure buy-in and alignment.

CLI Command to Implement Change Management:
bashCopy code
$ implement-change-management   --establish=change_control_process   --communicate=transparently

7. Failure to Plan for Maintenance and Support

Failure to plan for maintenance and support can result in the degradation of the data warehouse over time, as data quality issues arise, technology evolves, and business requirements change. To avoid this pitfall, organizations should develop a comprehensive maintenance plan that includes regular data quality checks, software updates, performance tuning, and user support. Planning for maintenance and support from the outset ensures that the data warehouse remains effective and reliable in the long term.

CLI Command to Plan Maintenance and Support:
bashCopy code

```
$          plan-maintenance-support          --
include=data_quality_checks,software_updates,performanc
e_tuning
```

By understanding and addressing common pitfalls in data warehousing projects, organizations can increase the likelihood of success and derive maximum value from their data assets. By focusing on requirements gathering, data quality, scope management, executive support, testing and validation, change management, and maintenance and support, organizations can mitigate risks, minimize disruptions, and achieve their goals effectively. By following best practices and leveraging appropriate strategies and techniques, organizations can ensure the success of their data warehousing projects and drive better business outcomes through data-driven decision-making.

Chapter 10: Emerging Trends and Future of Data Warehousing

Data warehousing has evolved significantly in recent years, driven by advancements in technology, changes in business requirements, and shifting industry dynamics. Next, we'll explore some of the current trends shaping the field of data warehousing, their implications, and how organizations can leverage them to drive innovation and achieve competitive advantage.

CLI Command to Explore Current Trends:

bashCopy code

```
$ explore-current-trends
```

1. Cloud-Based Data Warehousing

One of the most significant trends in data warehousing is the adoption of cloud-based solutions. Cloud data warehouses offer scalability, flexibility, and cost-effectiveness, allowing organizations to scale their infrastructure dynamically and pay only for the resources they use. With cloud-based data warehousing platforms such as Amazon Redshift, Google BigQuery, and Snowflake, organizations can store and analyze massive volumes of data without the need for extensive on-premises infrastructure.

CLI Command to Deploy Cloud-Based Data Warehousing:

bashCopy code

```
$           deploy-cloud-data-warehousing           --
platform=Amazon_Redshift
```

2. Data Lake Integration

Another emerging trend is the integration of data lakes with traditional data warehouses. Data lakes provide a centralized repository for storing raw, unstructured, and semi-structured data, while data warehouses offer structured, curated, and optimized data for analysis. By integrating data lakes with data warehouses, organizations can leverage the strengths of both approaches to gain deeper insights, improve data governance, and support a wider range of analytics use cases.

CLI Command to Integrate Data Lake with Data Warehouse:
bashCopy code

$ integrate-data-lake-with-data-warehouse

3. Real-Time Data Processing

Real-time data processing is becoming increasingly important as organizations seek to make faster, more informed decisions based on up-to-date information. Traditional batch processing approaches are being replaced by real-time streaming architectures that enable continuous data ingestion, processing, and analysis. Technologies such as Apache Kafka, Apache Flink, and Apache Spark Streaming are being used to build real-time data pipelines that deliver actionable insights in near real-time.

CLI Command to Implement Real-Time Data Processing:
bashCopy code

$ implement-real-time-data-processing --technology=Apache_Kafka

4. Machine Learning and AI Integration

Machine learning and artificial intelligence (AI) are being integrated into data warehousing platforms to automate tasks, uncover hidden patterns, and generate predictive insights. Organizations are leveraging machine learning algorithms for tasks such as anomaly detection, pattern recognition, and recommendation engines to enhance decision-making and drive innovation. With tools such as Amazon SageMaker, Google AI Platform, and Microsoft Azure Machine Learning, organizations can build and deploy machine learning models directly within their data warehousing environment.

CLI Command to Integrate Machine Learning and AI:
bashCopy code

```
$              integrate-machine-learning-ai          --
platform=Google_AI_Platform
```

5. Data Democratization

Data democratization is a trend aimed at making data more accessible and usable to a wider audience within organizations. Instead of relying solely on data specialists or IT departments, organizations are empowering business users, analysts, and decision-makers to access, analyze, and visualize data independently. Self-service analytics tools such as Tableau, Power BI, and Looker are enabling users to explore data, create reports, and derive insights without the need for technical expertise.

CLI Command to Implement Data Democratization:
bashCopy code

```
$              implement-data-democratization          --
tools=Power_BI,Tableau,Looker
```

6. Edge Computing

Edge computing is gaining traction in data warehousing as organizations seek to process and analyze data closer to the source of data generation. By moving computing resources closer to IoT devices, sensors, and other data-generating endpoints, organizations can reduce latency, improve data privacy and security, and support real-time analytics use cases. Edge computing platforms such as AWS IoT Greengrass and Microsoft Azure IoT Edge are enabling organizations to deploy data warehousing solutions at the edge of their networks.

CLI Command to Deploy Edge Computing for Data Warehousing:

```bash
bashCopy code
$ deploy-edge-computing --platform=AWS_IoT_Greengrass
```

These trends are reshaping the landscape of data warehousing, driving innovation, and opening up new opportunities for organizations to derive insights and create value from their data assets. By embracing cloud-based data warehousing, integrating data lakes, adopting real-time data processing, integrating machine learning and AI, promoting data democratization, and leveraging edge computing, organizations can stay ahead of the curve and unlock the full potential of their data to drive business growth and innovation.

Future Directions and Innovations in Data Warehousing

The field of data warehousing is constantly evolving, driven by advancements in technology, changes in business requirements, and emerging industry trends. Next, we'll explore some of the future directions and innovations shaping the future of data warehousing, their potential impact, and how organizations can prepare for these changes to stay ahead of the curve.

CLI Command to Explore Future Directions and Innovations:

```bash
bashCopy code
$ explore-future-directions-innovations
```

1. Augmented Analytics

Augmented analytics is an emerging trend that combines machine learning, natural language processing, and other advanced techniques to automate data preparation, analysis, and insight generation. By leveraging augmented analytics tools, organizations can empower business users to derive insights from data more easily and quickly, without requiring specialized data analysis skills. Augmented analytics platforms such as ThoughtSpot, DataRobot, and IBM Watson are poised to revolutionize the way organizations use data to drive decision-making.

CLI Command to Implement Augmented Analytics:

bashCopy code

```
$ implement-augmented-analytics --platform=ThoughtSpot
```

2. Quantum Computing

Quantum computing represents a paradigm shift in data processing capabilities, offering the potential to solve complex problems that are currently intractable with classical computing methods. In the context of data warehousing, quantum computing holds the promise of dramatically accelerating data processing, optimization, and machine learning tasks. While quantum computing is still in its early stages, organizations are beginning to explore its potential applications in data warehousing and analytics.

CLI Command to Explore Quantum Computing:

bashCopy code

```
$ explore-quantum-computing
```

3. Blockchain Technology

Blockchain technology is gaining traction as a means of enhancing data security, integrity, and transparency in data warehousing and analytics. By leveraging blockchain-based solutions, organizations can create immutable, tamper-proof records of data transactions, ensuring the integrity and authenticity of data stored in the data warehouse. Blockchain technology also has the potential to streamline data sharing and collaboration among multiple stakeholders while maintaining data privacy and security.

CLI Command to Implement Blockchain Technology:

bashCopy code

```
$ implement-blockchain-technology
```

4. Explainable AI

Explainable AI is an emerging area of research focused on making machine learning models more transparent, interpretable, and understandable to human users. In the context of data warehousing, explainable AI techniques enable organizations to gain insights into how machine learning models make predictions and recommendations, allowing them to trust and validate the results more effectively. Explainable AI tools such as IBM AI Explainability 360 and Google Cloud Explainable AI are enabling organizations to deploy machine learning models with greater confidence and transparency.

CLI Command to Implement Explainable AI:

bashCopy code

```
$              implement-explainable-ai              --tool=IBM_AI_Explainability_360
```

5. Automated Data Management

Automated data management is a future direction in data warehousing aimed at streamlining and simplifying the process of data ingestion, integration, transformation, and governance. By leveraging automation technologies such as robotic process automation (RPA), organizations can reduce manual effort, minimize errors, and accelerate time-to-insight. Automated data management tools such as Informatica, Talend, and Apache Nifi are enabling organizations to automate repetitive data management tasks and focus on higher-value activities.

CLI Command to Implement Automated Data Management:

bashCopy code

```
$         implement-automated-data-management         --tool=Informatica
```

6. Data Mesh Architecture

Data mesh architecture is an innovative approach to data warehousing that emphasizes decentralized data ownership, domain-driven data products, and self-serve data infrastructure. Instead of relying on a centralized data warehouse, data mesh architecture distributes data management responsibilities across decentralized teams or domains, enabling faster innovation, greater agility, and better alignment with business objectives. Organizations are beginning to explore data mesh architecture as a way to overcome the limitations of traditional data warehousing approaches and unlock the full potential of their data assets.

CLI Command to Implement Data Mesh Architecture:

bashCopy code

```
$ implement-data-mesh-architecture
```

These future directions and innovations are reshaping the future of data warehousing, offering new opportunities for organizations to derive insights, drive innovation, and achieve competitive advantage. By embracing augmented analytics, quantum computing, blockchain technology, explainable AI, automated data management, and data mesh architecture, organizations can prepare for the future of data warehousing and position themselves for success in the digital era. By staying abreast of emerging trends and innovations, organizations can leverage the full potential of their data assets to drive business growth and innovation.

BOOK 2
MASTERING DATA MODELING FOR DATA WAREHOUSING

ROB BOTWRIGHT

Chapter 1: Introduction to Data Modeling in Data Warehousing

Data modeling is a fundamental aspect of data warehousing, essential for organizing, structuring, and representing data in a meaningful way. Next, we delve into the core concepts of data modeling, including its importance, key techniques, and best practices for implementation.

CLI Command to Explore Data Modeling Concepts:

bashCopy code

$ explore-data-modeling-concepts

1. Importance of Data Modeling

Data modeling plays a crucial role in the success of data warehousing projects by providing a blueprint for organizing and structuring data. It helps stakeholders understand the relationships between different data elements, define business rules, and ensure data consistency and integrity. By capturing the semantics of the data in a formalized manner, data modeling facilitates effective communication between business users, data analysts, and IT professionals, leading to more accurate and reliable decision-making.

CLI Command to Define Data Model:

bashCopy code

$ define-data-model --tool=ERWin

2. Entity-Relationship Modeling

Entity-Relationship (ER) modeling is a widely used technique for representing the relationships between different entities or objects in a data model. In ER modeling, entities are represented as tables, attributes as columns, and relationships as lines connecting entities. The cardinality and degree of relationships are defined to specify how entities are related to each other. ER modeling provides a visual representation of the data model, making it easier to understand and communicate.

CLI Command to Create Entity-Relationship Model:
bashCopy code

```
$ create-er-model --tool=Lucidchart
```

3. Dimensional Modeling

Dimensional modeling is a specialized technique used primarily in data warehousing to organize and structure data for analytical purposes. In dimensional modeling, data is organized into two types of tables: fact tables and dimension tables. Fact tables contain quantitative data, such as sales transactions or inventory levels, while dimension tables contain descriptive attributes, such as product names or customer demographics. Dimensional modeling simplifies complex data relationships and enables faster query performance for analytical queries.

CLI Command to Implement Dimensional Model:
bashCopy code

```
$ implement-dimensional-model --tool=StarSchemaDesigner
```

4. Normalization and Denormalization

Normalization is the process of organizing data in a relational database to reduce redundancy and improve data integrity. It involves decomposing tables into smaller, more atomic entities and establishing relationships between them. Denormalization, on the other hand, involves combining normalized tables to improve query performance by reducing the number of joins required. The choice between normalization and denormalization depends on factors such as query patterns, performance requirements, and data consistency considerations.

CLI Command to Normalize Data:
bashCopy code

```
$ normalize-data --technique=ThirdNormalForm
```

CLI Command to Denormalize Data:
bashCopy code

```
$ denormalize-data --technique=StarSchema
```

5. Hierarchical Modeling

Hierarchical modeling is a data modeling technique used to represent hierarchical relationships between data elements. It is commonly used in hierarchical databases and XML data structures, where data is organized in a tree-like structure with parent-child relationships. Hierarchical modeling is well-suited for representing nested data structures, such as organizational charts, file systems, or product categories.

CLI Command to Implement Hierarchical Model:
bashCopy code

```
$ implement-hierarchical-model --tool=XMLSpy
```

6. Data Warehousing Best Practices

In addition to understanding the core concepts of data modeling, it's essential to follow best practices to ensure the success of data warehousing projects. Some key best practices include involving stakeholders early in the process, defining clear business requirements, maintaining data quality, documenting the data model comprehensively, and conducting regular reviews and updates to accommodate changes in business needs.

CLI Command to Implement Data Warehousing Best Practices:
bashCopy code

```
$ implement-data-warehousing-best-practices
```

Understanding data modeling concepts is essential for designing effective data warehousing solutions that meet the needs of business users and support data-driven decision-making. By mastering techniques such as entity-relationship modeling, dimensional modeling, normalization, denormalization, and hierarchical modeling, organizations can create robust and scalable data models that facilitate efficient data storage, retrieval, and analysis. By following best practices and leveraging appropriate tools and techniques, organizations can harness the full potential of their data assets and drive business growth and innovation.

Importance of Data Modeling in Data Warehousing

Data modeling is a foundational aspect of data warehousing, playing a crucial role in the success and effectiveness of data-driven initiatives within organizations. Next, we'll delve into the significance of data modeling in data warehousing, exploring its role in organizing, structuring, and optimizing data for analytical purposes.

CLI Command to Explore the Importance of Data Modeling:

bashCopy code

```
$ explore-data-modeling-importance
```

1. Organizing Complex Data Structures

One of the primary reasons for the importance of data modeling in data warehousing is its ability to organize complex data structures into a logical and coherent framework. In today's data-driven world, organizations deal with vast amounts of data coming from various sources, including transactional systems, IoT devices, social media, and more. Data modeling provides a structured approach to organizing this data, making it easier to understand, manage, and analyze.

CLI Command to Organize Data Structures:

bashCopy code

```
$ organize-data-structures --tool=ERStudio
```

2. Facilitating Effective Communication

Data modeling serves as a common language that enables effective communication between different stakeholders involved in data warehousing projects. Business users, data analysts, data scientists, and IT professionals often have different perspectives and requirements when it comes to data. Data modeling helps bridge these gaps by providing a visual representation of the data model, allowing stakeholders to collaborate more effectively and ensure alignment with business objectives.

CLI Command to Communicate Data Models:

bashCopy code

```
$ communicate-data-models --tool=Lucidchart
```

3. Enhancing Data Quality and Integrity

Data modeling plays a critical role in ensuring data quality and integrity within a data warehouse. By defining clear relationships, constraints, and business rules, data modeling helps maintain data consistency and accuracy over time. It enables organizations to enforce data quality standards, identify and resolve inconsistencies, and prevent data anomalies that could compromise the reliability of analytical insights derived from the data.

CLI Command to Ensure Data Quality:

bashCopy code

```
$ ensure-data-quality --tool=Talend
```

4. Supporting Scalability and Performance

Data modeling is essential for designing data warehouses that are scalable and performant, capable of handling large volumes of data and supporting complex analytical queries. By employing techniques such as dimensional modeling and indexing, data modeling enables organizations to optimize data storage, retrieval, and query execution. It ensures that data warehouses can scale to accommodate growing data volumes and deliver responsive performance for analytical workloads.

CLI Command to Optimize Data Warehouses:

bashCopy code

```
$ optimize-data-warehouses --technique=DimensionalModeling
```

5. Enabling Agile Development and Iterative Design

Data modeling facilitates agile development practices and iterative design methodologies in data warehousing projects. By breaking down complex requirements into smaller, more manageable components, data modeling allows organizations to iterate quickly, gather feedback from stakeholders, and adapt the data model as needed. It supports a flexible and iterative approach to data warehousing that aligns with the dynamic nature of business requirements and evolving data sources.

CLI Command to Implement Agile Data Modeling:

bashCopy code

$ implement-agile-data-modeling --methodology=Scrum

6. Driving Business Insights and Decision-Making

Ultimately, the importance of data modeling in data warehousing lies in its ability to drive business insights and decision-making. By organizing and structuring data in a way that is meaningful and relevant to the business, data modeling enables organizations to derive actionable insights, uncover hidden patterns, and make informed decisions based on data-driven evidence. It empowers organizations to extract maximum value from their data assets and gain a competitive edge in the marketplace.

CLI Command to Derive Business Insights:

bashCopy code

$ derive-business-insights --tool=Tableau

In summary, data modeling plays a vital role in data warehousing by organizing complex data structures, facilitating effective communication, enhancing data quality and integrity, supporting scalability and performance, enabling agile development, and driving business insights and decision-making. By understanding the importance of data modeling and investing in robust data modeling practices, organizations can unlock the full potential of their data assets and achieve success in their data warehousing initiatives.

Chapter 2: The Basics of Entity-Relationship Modeling

Entity-Relationship (ER) diagrams are a fundamental tool in the field of data modeling, serving as visual representations of the relationships between entities within a database. Next, we explore the significance of ER diagrams, their components, and how they contribute to the design and understanding of relational databases.

CLI Command to Explore Entity-Relationship Diagrams:
bashCopy code

```
$ explore-er-diagrams
```

1. Understanding Entity-Relationship Diagrams

ER diagrams are graphical representations that depict the entities, attributes, and relationships within a database schema. They provide a visual means of understanding the structure of a database, including the entities (objects or concepts), attributes (properties or characteristics), and relationships (associations or connections) between entities. ER diagrams are invaluable tools for database designers, developers, and stakeholders, as they facilitate communication, collaboration, and comprehension of complex data models.

CLI Command to Create an ER Diagram:
bashCopy code

```
$ create-er-diagram --tool=Lucidchart
```

2. Components of ER Diagrams

ER diagrams consist of several key components, each representing different aspects of the database schema:

Entities: Entities represent objects or concepts in the real world, such as customers, products, or orders. They are depicted as rectangles in ER diagrams.

Attributes: Attributes describe the properties or characteristics of entities, such as name, age, or address. They are represented as ovals connected to their respective entities.

Relationships: Relationships define the associations or connections between entities. They indicate how entities are related to each other and are represented as lines connecting entities.

CLI Command to Define ER Diagram Components:

bashCopy code

$ define-er-diagram-components

3. Types of Relationships

ER diagrams depict different types of relationships between entities, including:

One-to-One (1:1): A single instance of one entity is related to a single instance of another entity.

One-to-Many (1:N): A single instance of one entity is related to multiple instances of another entity.

Many-to-One (N:1): Multiple instances of one entity are related to a single instance of another entity.

Many-to-Many (N:M): Multiple instances of one entity are related to multiple instances of another entity.

These relationships are represented graphically in ER diagrams using appropriate symbols and cardinality indicators.

CLI Command to Model Relationships in ER Diagrams:

bashCopy code

$ model-relationships-in-er-diagrams

4. Role of ER Diagrams in Database Design

ER diagrams play a crucial role in the database design process, aiding in the conceptual, logical, and physical design phases. In the conceptual design phase, ER diagrams help capture the requirements and constraints of the database environment, providing a high-level view of the data model. In the logical design phase, ER diagrams are refined to include additional details such as data types, keys, and constraints, resulting in a more detailed representation of the database schema. In the physical design phase, ER diagrams are translated into a database implementation, specifying tables, columns, indexes, and other database objects.

CLI Command to Design Databases Using ER Diagrams:
bashCopy code

```
$ design-databases-using-er-diagrams
```

5. Tools for Creating ER Diagrams

There are various tools available for creating ER diagrams, ranging from simple drawing tools to sophisticated database design tools. Some popular tools include Lucidchart, Microsoft Visio, draw.io, and ER/Studio. These tools provide a user-friendly interface for designing, editing, and sharing ER diagrams, along with features such as automatic layout, entity relationship notation, and export options.

CLI Command to Select ER Diagram Creation Tool:
bashCopy code

```
$ select-er-diagram-creation-tool --tool=Lucidchart
```

6. Best Practices for Using ER Diagrams

To maximize the effectiveness of ER diagrams, it's essential to follow best practices such as:

Keep it simple: Focus on capturing the essential entities, attributes, and relationships without overcomplicating the diagram.

Use consistent naming conventions: Maintain consistency in naming entities, attributes, and relationships to improve clarity and understanding.

Document assumptions and constraints: Provide annotations and notes to document any assumptions or constraints that are not evident from the diagram itself.

Validate with stakeholders: Collaborate with stakeholders to validate the ER diagram and ensure it accurately reflects the requirements and expectations of the database environment.

CLI Command to Implement ER Diagram Best Practices:
bashCopy code

```
$ implement-er-diagram-best-practices
```

In summary, Entity-Relationship diagrams are invaluable tools for designing, communicating, and understanding the structure of relational databases. By providing visual representations of entities, attributes, and relationships, ER diagrams facilitate collaboration, promote clarity, and guide the database design process from conceptualization to implementation. By mastering the concepts and techniques of ER diagramming, database designers and developers can create robust, scalable, and efficient database schemas that meet the needs of their organizations.

Relationship Types and Cardinality

In the realm of database design, understanding relationship types and cardinality is paramount. These concepts delineate the connections between entities within a database, offering insights into how data is structured and interconnected. This chapter delves into the significance of relationship types and cardinality, elucidating their role in database design and providing practical insights into their deployment.

CLI Command to Explore Relationship Types and Cardinality:

bashCopy code

$ explore-relationship-types-cardinality

1. Relationship Types

Relationship types delineate the nature of the connections between entities within a database. There are several common relationship types, each with distinct characteristics:

One-to-One (1:1): In a one-to-one relationship, each record in one entity is associated with exactly one record in another entity, and vice versa. This type of relationship is relatively rare in database design but can be useful in scenarios where entities have a one-to-one correspondence.

One-to-Many (1:N): In a one-to-many relationship, each record in one entity can be associated with multiple records in another entity, but each record in the second entity is associated with only one record in the first entity. This type of relationship is common in many real-world scenarios, such as a customer having multiple orders.

Many-to-One (N:1): In a many-to-one relationship, multiple records in one entity are associated with a single record in another entity. This type of relationship is essentially the inverse of a one-to-many relationship and is often encountered in scenarios where multiple entities are related to a single parent entity.

Many-to-Many (N:M): In a many-to-many relationship, multiple records in one entity can be associated with multiple records in another entity. This type of relationship requires the introduction of a junction table to facilitate the many-to-many relationship, as it cannot be directly represented in relational databases.

CLI Command to Define Relationship Types:

bashCopy code

```
$ define-relationship-types
```

2. Cardinality

Cardinality refers to the numerical relationship between instances of one entity and instances of another entity in a specific relationship type. Cardinality is typically expressed using cardinality ratios, which indicate the minimum and maximum number of instances of one entity that can be associated with instances of another entity.

Minimum Cardinality: The minimum number of instances of one entity that must be associated with instances of another entity in a specific relationship type. It denotes the lower bound of the relationship.

Maximum Cardinality: The maximum number of instances of one entity that can be associated with instances of another entity in a specific relationship type. It denotes the upper bound of the relationship.

CLI Command to Determine Cardinality:

bashCopy code

```
$ determine-cardinality
```

3. Practical Examples

To elucidate these concepts, let's consider some practical examples:

One-to-One Relationship: A person may have only one social security number, and a social security number is associated with only one person. This represents a one-to-one relationship.

One-to-Many Relationship: A customer can place multiple orders, but each order is associated with only one customer. This exemplifies a one-to-many relationship.

Many-to-One Relationship: Multiple students may enroll in the same course, but each student is enrolled in only one course. This illustrates a many-to-one relationship.

Many-to-Many Relationship: A student can attend multiple classes, and a class may have multiple students enrolled. This showcases a many-to-many relationship, which necessitates the use of a junction table to resolve it.

CLI Command to Model Relationship Types:

bashCopy code

$ model-relationship-types --tool=Lucidchart

4. Importance in Database Design

Relationship types and cardinality are indispensable in database design, as they inform the structure and integrity of the database schema. By delineating the connections between entities and specifying the constraints governing these relationships, database designers ensure data integrity, prevent anomalies, and facilitate efficient querying and data manipulation operations.

CLI Command to Implement Relationship Types and Cardinality:

bashCopy code

$ implement-relationship-types-cardinality

5. Best Practices

To leverage relationship types and cardinality effectively in database design, adhere to best practices such as:

Clearly define and document relationship types and cardinality constraints during the database design phase.

Validate relationship types and cardinality with stakeholders to ensure alignment with business requirements.

Regularly review and refine relationship types and cardinality as the database evolves to accommodate changing business needs and data requirements.

CLI Command to Implement Best Practices:

bashCopy code

$ implement-relationship-types-cardinality-best-practices

In summary, relationship types and cardinality are integral components of database design, delineating the connections between entities and governing the integrity of the database schema. By understanding and appropriately deploying these concepts, database designers can create robust, efficient, and scalable database schemas that effectively model real-world relationships and support the data management needs of organizations.

Chapter 3: Dimensional Modeling Principles and Techniques

Dimensional modeling is a critical technique in the realm of data warehousing, enabling efficient and effective organization of data for analytical purposes. This chapter delves into the fundamentals of dimensional modeling, exploring its key concepts, components, and best practices for implementation.

CLI Command to Explore Dimensional Modeling Fundamentals:

bashCopy code

```
$ explore-dimensional-modeling-fundamentals
```

1. Understanding Dimensional Modeling

Dimensional modeling is a technique used to structure and organize data in a way that facilitates easy and efficient querying and analysis. Unlike traditional relational modeling, which focuses on normalizing data to eliminate redundancy, dimensional modeling emphasizes simplicity and ease of use for analytical purposes. It involves organizing data into two primary types of tables: fact tables and dimension tables.

CLI Command to Define Dimensional Modeling:

bashCopy code

```
$ define-dimensional-modeling
```

2. Fact Tables

Fact tables are central to dimensional modeling and contain quantitative data, also known as facts or measures, that represent business transactions or events. Fact tables typically have foreign key relationships with one or more dimension tables, which provide context and descriptive attributes for the facts stored in the fact table. Common examples of fact tables include sales transactions, inventory levels, and financial metrics.

CLI Command to Create Fact Tables:

bashCopy code

$ create-fact-tables

3. Dimension Tables

Dimension tables provide descriptive context for the data stored in fact tables by capturing the attributes or characteristics associated with the facts. These attributes are known as dimensions and represent the various perspectives or viewpoints by which the data can be analyzed. Dimension tables typically contain descriptive attributes such as product names, customer demographics, time periods, and geographical locations.

CLI Command to Create Dimension Tables:

bashCopy code

$ create-dimension-tables

4. Star Schema vs. Snowflake Schema

Two common dimensional modeling schemas are the star schema and the snowflake schema. In a star schema, all dimension tables are directly connected to the fact table, forming a star-like structure. This simplifies query performance but can lead to redundancy in dimension tables. In contrast, a snowflake schema normalizes dimension tables by splitting them into multiple related tables, reducing redundancy but potentially complicating query performance.

CLI Command to Implement Star Schema:

bashCopy code

$ implement-star-schema

CLI Command to Implement Snowflake Schema:

bashCopy code

$ implement-snowflake-schema

5. Benefits of Dimensional Modeling

Dimensional modeling offers several benefits for data warehousing and analytical purposes:

Simplified querying: Dimensional modeling simplifies querying and analysis by organizing data into intuitive and easy-to-understand structures.

Improved performance: By denormalizing data and optimizing query paths, dimensional modeling can significantly improve query performance for analytical workloads.

Enhanced usability: Dimensional models are designed with end-users in mind, providing intuitive access to data for reporting, analysis, and decision-making.

Scalability: Dimensional models are inherently scalable and flexible, allowing organizations to adapt to changing data requirements and business needs over time.

CLI Command to Implement Dimensional Modeling Benefits:

bashCopy code

$ implement-dimensional-modeling-benefits

6. Best Practices

To leverage dimensional modeling effectively, adhere to best practices such as:

Start with business requirements: Begin by understanding the analytical requirements and business goals that the dimensional model needs to support.

Design for usability: Focus on creating dimensional models that are intuitive and easy to use for end-users, ensuring they can derive value from the data.

Normalize where appropriate: While dimensional modeling often involves denormalizing data for performance, there may be cases where normalization is necessary to maintain data integrity or reduce redundancy.

Iterate and refine: Continuously iterate and refine the dimensional model based on feedback from stakeholders and evolving business needs.

CLI Command to Implement Dimensional Modeling Best Practices:

bashCopy code

```
$ implement-dimensional-modeling-best-practices
```

In summary, dimensional modeling is a fundamental technique for organizing data in a way that supports efficient querying and analysis in data warehousing environments. By understanding the principles and best practices of dimensional modeling, organizations can create robust, scalable, and user-friendly dimensional models that empower users to derive valuable insights and make informed decisions based on their data.

Star Schema vs. Snowflake Schema

In the realm of data warehousing, choosing the appropriate schema is paramount for ensuring optimal performance, scalability, and ease of querying. Two commonly employed schemas are the star schema and the snowflake schema. This chapter elucidates the nuances between these schemas, their advantages, disadvantages, and considerations for deployment.

CLI Command to Explore Star Schema vs. Snowflake Schema:

bashCopy code

```
$ explore-star-snowflake-schema
```

1. Star Schema

The star schema is a simple, denormalized schema that features a central fact table surrounded by dimension tables, resembling a star-like structure. In this schema, each dimension table is directly connected to the fact table through foreign key relationships, enabling straightforward and efficient querying. The star schema simplifies data retrieval, enhances query performance, and is well-suited for analytical workloads with predictable query patterns.

CLI Command to Deploy Star Schema:

bashCopy code

$ deploy-star-schema

2. Snowflake Schema

In contrast, the snowflake schema is a normalized schema that extends the star schema by further normalizing dimension tables into sub-dimension tables. This results in a more complex, multi-level hierarchy resembling a snowflake. While the snowflake schema reduces data redundancy and conserves storage space, it can complicate query performance due to the need for additional joins across multiple tables. However, the snowflake schema excels in scenarios where data integrity and consistency are paramount, such as highly normalized transactional databases.

CLI Command to Deploy Snowflake Schema:

bashCopy code

$ deploy-snowflake-schema

3. Advantages of Star Schema

Simplified querying: The star schema's denormalized structure simplifies querying by reducing the number of joins required to retrieve data.

Enhanced performance: With fewer joins and optimized query paths, star schemas often deliver superior query performance for analytical workloads.

Intuitive design: The straightforward design of star schemas makes them easy to understand, maintain, and scale as data volumes grow.

CLI Command to Explore Star Schema Advantages:
bashCopy code
$ explore-star-schema-advantages

4. Advantages of Snowflake Schema

Data integrity: By normalizing dimension tables, snowflake schemas maintain data integrity and consistency, reducing the risk of data anomalies.

Storage efficiency: Normalization in snowflake schemas conserves storage space by eliminating redundant data and minimizing data duplication.

Flexibility: Snowflake schemas offer greater flexibility for accommodating changes to the data model, allowing for easier schema evolution over time.

CLI Command to Explore Snowflake Schema Advantages:
bashCopy code
$ explore-snowflake-schema-advantages

5. Considerations for Deployment

When deciding between a star schema and a snowflake schema, several factors should be considered:

Query performance: Evaluate the query performance requirements of the analytical workloads and consider the trade-offs between simplicity (star schema) and normalization (snowflake schema).

Data complexity: Assess the complexity of the data model, including the number of dimensions, cardinality, and relationships, to determine the most suitable schema for the data.

Maintenance overhead: Consider the overhead associated with maintaining and managing the schema, including data loading, indexing, and schema evolution.

CLI Command to Consider Deployment Factors:
bashCopy code
$ consider-deployment-factors

6. Best Practices

To leverage star schemas and snowflake schemas effectively, adhere to best practices such as:

Start with business requirements: Begin by understanding the analytical requirements and business goals that the schema needs to support.

Prototype and test: Prototype both schema types and conduct performance testing to evaluate their suitability for the workload.

Monitor and optimize: Continuously monitor query performance and optimize the schema as needed to ensure optimal performance and scalability.

CLI Command to Implement Best Practices:

bashCopy code

```
$ implement-schema-best-practices
```

In summary, the choice between a star schema and a snowflake schema depends on various factors, including query performance requirements, data complexity, and maintenance overhead. By understanding the nuances between these schemas and considering deployment factors and best practices, organizations can make informed decisions and design data warehousing solutions that meet their analytical needs effectively.

Chapter 4: Fact Tables and Dimension Tables Design

In the realm of data warehousing, fact tables serve as the cornerstone for storing quantitative data representing business events or transactions. Designing fact tables is a crucial aspect of creating an effective data warehouse, as it determines how data is organized, stored, and queried. This chapter delves into the intricacies of designing fact tables, exploring key considerations, best practices, and practical insights for implementation.

CLI Command to Explore Designing Fact Tables:

bashCopy code

$ explore-designing-fact-tables

1. Understanding Fact Tables

Fact tables are central to dimensional modeling and typically store numeric, additive data known as facts or measures. These facts represent the metrics, quantities, or events that are being analyzed in the data warehouse. Fact tables contain foreign key relationships with dimension tables, providing context and descriptive attributes for the facts stored within.

CLI Command to Define Fact Tables:

bashCopy code

$ define-fact-tables

2. Key Components of Fact Tables

When designing fact tables, several key components need to be considered:

Fact table granularity: Granularity refers to the level of detail or aggregation at which data is stored in the fact table. It is essential to determine the appropriate granularity based on the analytical requirements and querying patterns.

Fact table columns: Fact tables typically contain columns representing the various facts or measures being analyzed. These columns may include quantitative metrics such as sales revenue, quantities sold, or transaction amounts.

Foreign key relationships: Fact tables establish relationships with dimension tables through foreign key columns, which provide the necessary context and dimensions for analyzing the facts stored within.

CLI Command to Identify Fact Table Components:

bashCopy code

```
$ identify-fact-table-components
```

3. Types of Fact Tables

There are several types of fact tables, each catering to different analytical requirements:

Transactional fact tables: These fact tables store individual business transactions or events at the lowest level of granularity. They capture detailed information about each transaction, such as sales orders, invoices, or shipments.

Periodic snapshot fact tables: These fact tables capture aggregated data at regular intervals, such as daily, weekly, or monthly summaries. They are useful for tracking performance metrics over time, such as sales revenue by month or customer activity by quarter.

Accumulating snapshot fact tables: These fact tables track the progress or status of a process or workflow over time. They store snapshots of the process at different stages, allowing for analysis of process efficiency and bottlenecks.

CLI Command to Create Different Types of Fact Tables:

bashCopy code

```
$ create-transactional-fact-table $ create-periodic-snapshot-fact-table $ create-accumulating-snapshot-fact-table
```

4. Best Practices for Fact Table Design

To design effective fact tables, adhere to best practices such as:

Choose the right granularity: Select the appropriate level of granularity for the fact table based on the analytical requirements and querying patterns.

Keep it simple: Avoid overcomplicating the fact table design by including only essential columns and maintaining a clear, intuitive structure.

Normalize where necessary: Normalize the fact table structure to reduce redundancy and improve data integrity, especially in cases where multiple facts share common dimensions.

Optimize for performance: Design fact tables with performance in mind, including appropriate indexing, partitioning, and data compression techniques to enhance query performance.

CLI Command to Implement Fact Table Design Best Practices:

bashCopy code

$ implement-fact-table-design-best-practices

5. Practical Insights

Consider the following practical insights when designing fact tables:

Understand the business requirements: Collaborate closely with stakeholders to understand the analytical requirements and business goals that the fact table needs to support.

Prototype and iterate: Prototype different fact table designs and iterate based on feedback from users and stakeholders to ensure alignment with business needs.

Document assumptions and decisions: Document the design decisions, assumptions, and constraints associated with the fact table to maintain clarity and transparency throughout the development process.

CLI Command to Implement Practical Insights:
bashCopy code
$ implement-fact-table-design-practical-insights

In summary, designing fact tables is a critical aspect of creating an effective data warehousing solution. By understanding the key components, types, and best practices associated with fact table design, organizations can create robust, scalable, and efficient fact tables that support their analytical needs and empower users to derive valuable insights from their data.

Designing Dimension Tables
In the architecture of a data warehouse, dimension tables play a pivotal role in providing context and descriptive attributes for the quantitative data stored in fact tables. Effective design of dimension tables is crucial for organizing data in a way that facilitates efficient querying, analysis, and reporting. This chapter explores the intricacies of designing dimension tables, covering key considerations, best practices, and practical insights for implementation.
CLI Command to Explore Designing Dimension Tables:
bashCopy code
$ explore-designing-dimension-tables
1. Understanding Dimension Tables
Dimension tables are a fundamental component of dimensional modeling, representing the various attributes or dimensions by which the data can be analyzed. These attributes provide context and descriptive information for the quantitative data stored in fact tables. Dimension tables typically contain one record for each unique value of the dimension, such as product, customer, time, or geography.
CLI Command to Define Dimension Tables:

bashCopy code

$ define-dimension-tables

2. Key Components of Dimension Tables

When designing dimension tables, several key components need to be considered:

Primary key: Each dimension table should have a primary key column that uniquely identifies each record within the table.

Descriptive attributes: Dimension tables contain columns representing the descriptive attributes or dimensions by which the data can be analyzed. These attributes provide context and additional information for the quantitative data stored in fact tables.

Hierarchies: Dimension tables may include hierarchical relationships between attributes, such as product categories and subcategories or geographical regions and subregions.

CLI Command to Identify Dimension Table Components:

bashCopy code

$ identify-dimension-table-components

3. Types of Dimension Tables

There are several types of dimension tables, each catering to different analytical requirements:

Conformed dimensions: These dimension tables are shared across multiple fact tables and provide consistent, standardized attributes for analysis. Conformed dimensions ensure data consistency and enable cross-functional analysis across different areas of the business.

Slowly changing dimensions (SCDs): Slowly changing dimensions capture changes to dimensional attributes over time. There are different types of SCDs, including Type 1 (overwrite), Type 2 (add new row), and Type 3 (add new column), each suited to different scenarios based on the nature of the data changes.

Junk dimensions: Junk dimensions consolidate low-cardinality, non-hierarchical attributes into a single dimension table to reduce the number of dimension tables in the data warehouse and simplify querying.

CLI Command to Create Different Types of Dimension Tables:

bashCopy code

$ create-conformed-dimension-table $ create-slowly-changing-dimension-table $ create-junk-dimension-table

4. Best Practices for Dimension Table Design

To design effective dimension tables, adhere to best practices such as:

Choose meaningful attributes: Include only meaningful, relevant attributes in the dimension table that provide valuable context for analyzing the data.

Normalize where necessary: Normalize the dimension table structure to reduce redundancy and improve data integrity, especially in cases where multiple dimension tables share common attributes.

Document metadata: Document metadata such as attribute definitions, data types, and source information to ensure clarity and transparency in the data warehouse.

CLI Command to Implement Dimension Table Design Best Practices:

bashCopy code

$ implement-dimension-table-design-best-practices

5. Practical Insights

Consider the following practical insights when designing dimension tables:

Understand the business requirements: Collaborate closely with stakeholders to understand the analytical requirements and business goals that the dimension table needs to support.

Prototype and iterate: Prototype different dimension table designs and iterate based on feedback from users and stakeholders to ensure alignment with business needs.

Standardize naming conventions: Establish standardized naming conventions for dimension table attributes to maintain consistency and clarity throughout the data warehouse.

CLI Command to Implement Practical Insights:

bashCopy code

```
$ implement-dimension-table-design-practical-insights
```

In summary, designing dimension tables is a critical aspect of creating an effective data warehousing solution. By understanding the key components, types, and best practices associated with dimension table design, organizations can create robust, scalable, and efficient dimension tables that support their analytical needs and empower users to derive valuable insights from their data.

Chapter 5: Advanced Data Modeling Techniques

Advanced Data Modeling Patterns

In the landscape of data modeling, advanced patterns go beyond the basics, offering sophisticated techniques to handle complex data structures and relationships. These patterns provide powerful solutions for modeling intricate business scenarios and optimizing data storage and retrieval. This chapter explores various advanced data modeling patterns, their applications, benefits, and practical implementation strategies.

CLI Command to Explore Advanced Data Modeling Patterns:

bashCopy code

```
$ explore-advanced-data-modeling-patterns
```

1. Hierarchical Modeling

Hierarchical modeling is a pattern used to represent hierarchical relationships between data entities, where each entity can have one or more parent or child entities. This pattern is commonly used to model organizational structures, product categories, geographical hierarchies, and other hierarchical data domains. Hierarchical modeling can be implemented using parent-child relationships or recursive relationships within the data model.

CLI Command to Implement Hierarchical Modeling:

bashCopy code

```
$ implement-hierarchical-modeling
```

2. Graph Modeling

Graph modeling is a pattern used to represent complex relationships between data entities using nodes and edges. Graph databases excel at modeling interconnected data with varying degrees of relationships, such as social networks, recommendation systems, and network analysis. Graph modeling allows for flexible querying and traversal of relationships, enabling advanced analytical insights and data discovery.

CLI Command to Implement Graph Modeling:

bashCopy code

$ implement-graph-modeling

3. Time Series Modeling

Time series modeling is a pattern used to analyze and forecast data over time, capturing temporal patterns, trends, and seasonality. Time series data often exhibits sequential dependencies and autocorrelation, making it suitable for specialized modeling techniques such as autoregressive integrated moving average (ARIMA), exponential smoothing (ETS), and seasonal decomposition. Time series modeling is widely used in forecasting demand, stock prices, weather patterns, and other time-dependent phenomena.

CLI Command to Implement Time Series Modeling:

bashCopy code

$ implement-time-series-modeling

4. Entity-Attribute-Value (EAV) Modeling

Entity-Attribute-Value (EAV) modeling is a pattern used to handle flexible or dynamic schemas where the attributes of entities can vary dynamically. In EAV modeling, data is stored in a flexible key-value format, allowing for the dynamic addition of new attributes without altering the underlying schema. While EAV modeling provides flexibility, it can lead to challenges in query performance, data integrity, and complexity in handling sparse data.

CLI Command to Implement EAV Modeling:

bashCopy code

$ implement-eav-modeling

5. Snowplow Schema

The Snowplow schema is a pattern used for event data modeling, capturing user interactions, behaviors, and events across digital platforms such as websites, mobile apps, and IoT devices. The Snowplow schema consists of four core tables: events, contexts, unstructured events, and derived contexts. This schema enables comprehensive tracking and analysis of user engagement, conversion funnels, and customer journeys across multiple touchpoints.

CLI Command to Implement Snowplow Schema:

bashCopy code

$ implement-snowplow-schema

6. Star Schema Extension

The Star Schema Extension pattern enhances the traditional star schema by incorporating additional tables or dimensions to capture more detailed or specialized aspects of the data. This pattern enables richer analysis and reporting by providing additional context and granularity to the data model. Common extensions include slowly changing dimensions (SCDs), bridge tables, and factless fact tables, which augment the star schema with additional dimensions or relationships.

CLI Command to Extend Star Schema:

bashCopy code

$ extend-star-schema

In summary, advanced data modeling patterns offer powerful solutions for handling complex data structures, relationships, and analytical requirements. By leveraging hierarchical modeling, graph modeling, time series modeling, EAV modeling, Snowplow schema, and star schema extension, organizations can design robust, scalable, and flexible data models that support their diverse analytical needs and enable actionable insights from their data.

Handling Slowly Changing Dimensions
Slowly changing dimensions (SCDs) are a fundamental aspect of data warehousing, addressing the need to capture and manage changes to dimensional attributes over time. As data evolves, dimensions such as product descriptions, customer demographics, and employee details may undergo modifications, necessitating effective strategies for handling these changes while maintaining data integrity and historical accuracy. This chapter delves into various techniques and best practices for handling slowly changing dimensions in data warehousing environments.

CLI Command to Explore Handling Slowly Changing Dimensions:
bashCopy code
$ explore-slowly-changing-dimensions

1. Understanding Slowly Changing Dimensions
Slowly changing dimensions refer to dimensions whose attributes change gradually over time, requiring tracking and management to preserve historical data accuracy. There are several types of slowly changing dimensions, categorized based on how they handle changes:

Type 1 (Overwrite): In Type 1 SCDs, changes to dimensional attributes are simply overwritten, with no historical tracking. This approach is suitable for attributes where historical values are not relevant or significant.

Type 2 (Add New Row): Type 2 SCDs create a new row in the dimension table for each change to a dimensional attribute, preserving historical data. This approach allows for tracking changes over time and maintaining historical accuracy.

Type 3 (Add New Column): Type 3 SCDs add new columns to the dimension table to store both the current and previous values of a dimensional attribute. While this approach provides limited historical tracking, it offers simplicity and efficiency for certain scenarios.

CLI Command to Define Slowly Changing Dimensions:

bashCopy code

```
$ define-slowly-changing-dimensions
```

2. Implementing Type 1 Slowly Changing Dimensions

Type 1 SCDs are relatively straightforward to implement, as they involve simply overwriting the existing attribute values with the new values. This approach is suitable for attributes where historical data is not critical, such as names or addresses. To deploy Type 1 SCDs, update the dimensional attribute directly with the new value whenever a change occurs.

CLI Command to Implement Type 1 Slowly Changing Dimensions:

bashCopy code

```
$ implement-type-1-scd
```

3. Implementing Type 2 Slowly Changing Dimensions

Type 2 SCDs are more complex to implement but offer comprehensive historical tracking of dimensional attribute changes. To deploy Type 2 SCDs, create a new row in the dimension table for each change to a dimensional attribute, including start and end dates to indicate the validity period of each record. This allows for accurate historical analysis and reporting.

CLI Command to Implement Type 2 Slowly Changing Dimensions:

bashCopy code

$ implement-type-2-scd

4. Implementing Type 3 Slowly Changing Dimensions

Type 3 SCDs strike a balance between simplicity and historical tracking by adding new columns to the dimension table to store both the current and previous values of a dimensional attribute. This approach provides limited historical tracking but can be more efficient for certain scenarios where full historical accuracy is not required.

CLI Command to Implement Type 3 Slowly Changing Dimensions:

bashCopy code

$ implement-type-3-scd

5. Best Practices for Handling Slowly Changing Dimensions

To effectively handle slowly changing dimensions, adhere to best practices such as:

Understand business requirements: Collaborate closely with stakeholders to understand the significance and impact of dimensional attribute changes on analytical reporting and decision-making.

Choose the appropriate SCD type: Select the most suitable SCD type based on the nature of the dimensional attributes and the analytical requirements of the data warehouse.

Document changes: Maintain documentation of dimensional attribute changes, including timestamps, reasons for change, and business context, to ensure transparency and auditability.

Implement auditing mechanisms: Implement auditing mechanisms to track changes to dimensional attributes and validate data integrity over time, ensuring accuracy and reliability of historical data.

CLI Command to Implement Best Practices for Handling SCDs:

bashCopy code

```
$ implement-scd-best-practices
```

In summary, handling slowly changing dimensions is a critical aspect of data warehousing, ensuring the accuracy, integrity, and historical tracking of dimensional attribute changes over time. By understanding the different types of slowly changing dimensions and implementing appropriate strategies and best practices, organizations can effectively manage changes to dimensional attributes and derive actionable insights from their data with confidence and reliability.

Chapter 6: Normalization and Denormalization Strategies

Normalization is a crucial concept in database design, aimed at minimizing data redundancy and dependency by organizing data into well-structured tables. By adhering to normalization principles, database designers can improve data integrity, reduce storage space, and enhance query performance. This chapter explores the fundamental concepts of normalization, including various normal forms, their applications, and practical implementation strategies.

CLI Command to Explore Normalization Concepts:

bashCopy code

$ explore-normalization-concepts

1. Understanding Normalization

Normalization is the process of organizing data in a database to reduce redundancy and dependency, ultimately improving data integrity and efficiency. The primary goal of normalization is to eliminate or minimize data anomalies such as update anomalies, insertion anomalies, and deletion anomalies, which can occur when data is not properly organized.

CLI Command to Define Normalization:

bashCopy code

$ define-normalization

2. The Normal Forms

There are several normal forms, each representing a specific level of data normalization. The most commonly discussed normal forms include:

First Normal Form (1NF): In 1NF, each column in a table contains atomic values, and there are no repeating groups of columns.

Second Normal Form (2NF): In 2NF, the table is in 1NF, and all non-key attributes are fully functionally dependent on the primary key.

Third Normal Form (3NF): In 3NF, the table is in 2NF, and there are no transitive dependencies between non-key attributes.

CLI Command to Describe Normal Forms:

bashCopy code

$ describe-normal-forms

3. Benefits of Normalization

Normalization offers several benefits, including:

Data integrity: By minimizing data redundancy and dependency, normalization reduces the risk of data anomalies and ensures consistent data representation.

Storage efficiency: Normalized databases typically require less storage space compared to denormalized databases, as redundant data is eliminated.

Query performance: Normalization can improve query performance by reducing the number of join operations required to retrieve data and by enabling more efficient indexing.

CLI Command to Highlight Benefits of Normalization:

bashCopy code

$ highlight-normalization-benefits

4. Practical Implementation Strategies

To implement normalization effectively, consider the following strategies:

Identify functional dependencies: Analyze the relationships between attributes in the data model to identify functional dependencies and determine the appropriate normalization level.

Normalize incrementally: Normalize the database schema incrementally, starting from the highest normal form and working downwards, to avoid over-normalization and maintain flexibility.

Denormalize selectively: While normalization is beneficial for data integrity and efficiency, selective denormalization may be necessary to optimize query performance in certain scenarios.

CLI Command to Implement Normalization Strategies:
bashCopy code

$ implement-normalization-strategies

5. Common Challenges and Pitfalls

Despite its benefits, normalization can also pose challenges and pitfalls, including:

Over-normalization: Excessive normalization can lead to complex data models, increased query complexity, and decreased performance.

Join overhead: Normalized databases may require more join operations to retrieve data, resulting in higher query execution times, especially for complex queries.

Balancing normalization and performance: Achieving the right balance between normalization and performance optimization requires careful consideration of the specific requirements and constraints of the application.

CLI Command to Address Common Challenges:
bashCopy code

$ address-normalization-challenges

In summary, normalization is a fundamental concept in database design, essential for ensuring data integrity, efficiency, and maintainability. By understanding the principles of normalization, applying appropriate normalization techniques, and addressing common challenges and pitfalls, database designers can create well-structured, efficient, and scalable databases that meet the needs of their applications and users.

Denormalization Strategies for Performance Optimization

Denormalization is a database optimization technique aimed at improving query performance by reintroducing redundancy into the database schema. By strategically duplicating and precalculating data, denormalization can reduce the need for complex join operations and improve data retrieval speed. This chapter explores various denormalization strategies, their applications, benefits, and practical implementation techniques.

CLI Command to Explore Denormalization Strategies:

bashCopy code

$ explore-denormalization-strategies

1. Understanding Denormalization

Denormalization involves deliberately introducing redundancy into the database schema to improve query performance. Unlike normalization, which aims to minimize redundancy and dependency, denormalization sacrifices some level of data integrity in favor of improved performance. By storing redundant data, denormalization reduces the need for join operations and simplifies query execution.

CLI Command to Define Denormalization:

bashCopy code

$ define-denormalization

2. Types of Denormalization

There are several types of denormalization, each catering to different performance optimization goals:

Materialized views: Materialized views store precomputed query results, allowing for fast data retrieval without the need for expensive join operations. Materialized views are particularly effective for aggregations, summaries, and frequently accessed queries.

Horizontal denormalization: Horizontal denormalization involves duplicating entire rows or subsets of rows from related tables into a single table. This approach simplifies querying by eliminating the need for joins but can lead to data redundancy and potential update anomalies.

Vertical denormalization: Vertical denormalization involves splitting a single table into multiple tables, each containing a subset of columns. This technique reduces the number of columns in each table, improving query performance by minimizing data access overhead.

CLI Command to Discuss Types of Denormalization:

bashCopy code

$ discuss-denormalization-types

3. Benefits of Denormalization

Denormalization offers several benefits for performance optimization:

Improved query performance: By reducing the need for join operations and minimizing data access overhead, denormalization can significantly improve query performance, especially for complex queries involving multiple tables.

Enhanced scalability: Denormalization can improve database scalability by reducing the computational load on the database server, allowing it to handle more concurrent user requests and larger datasets.

Simplified data access: Denormalized schemas simplify data access by eliminating the need for complex join operations, making it easier for developers and analysts to retrieve and manipulate data.

CLI Command to Highlight Benefits of Denormalization:
bashCopy code

$ highlight-denormalization-benefits

4. Practical Implementation Techniques

To implement denormalization effectively, consider the following techniques:

Identify performance bottlenecks: Analyze query execution plans and identify performance bottlenecks to determine which tables and queries would benefit most from denormalization.

Choose the right denormalization technique: Select the appropriate denormalization technique based on the specific performance optimization goals and requirements of the application.

Monitor and optimize: Continuously monitor database performance after denormalization and fine-tune the denormalized schema as needed to maintain optimal performance.

CLI Command to Implement Denormalization Techniques:
bashCopy code

$ implement-denormalization-techniques

5. Common Challenges and Pitfalls

Despite its benefits, denormalization can also pose challenges and pitfalls:

Data redundancy: Denormalization introduces redundancy into the database schema, increasing storage space and potentially leading to data inconsistency if updates are not properly managed.

Update anomalies: Redundant data in denormalized schemas can result in update anomalies, where changes to one copy of the data are not reflected in other copies, leading to data inconsistency.

Maintenance overhead: Denormalized schemas may require more complex maintenance and data synchronization processes to ensure data integrity and consistency over time.

CLI Command to Address Common Challenges:

bashCopy code

```
$ address-denormalization-challenges
```

In summary, denormalization is a powerful technique for optimizing database performance by reintroducing redundancy into the database schema. By strategically duplicating and precalculating data, denormalization can significantly improve query performance, scalability, and data access speed. However, it is essential to carefully consider the trade-offs and challenges associated with denormalization and implement appropriate techniques to mitigate potential risks and ensure data integrity and consistency.

Chapter 7: Modeling Hierarchies and Aggregations

Hierarchical modeling is a fundamental concept in database design, used to represent data relationships in a hierarchical structure. This chapter explores various hierarchical modeling techniques, their applications, benefits, and practical implementation strategies.

CLI Command to Explore Hierarchical Modeling Techniques:

bashCopy code

```
$ explore-hierarchical-modeling-techniques
```

1. Understanding Hierarchical Modeling

Hierarchical modeling organizes data into a tree-like structure, where each entity has a single parent and zero or more children. This model is suitable for representing data relationships with a clear hierarchy, such as organizational structures, file systems, product categories, and taxonomies.

CLI Command to Define Hierarchical Modeling:

bashCopy code

```
$ define-hierarchical-modeling
```

2. Types of Hierarchical Modeling

There are several types of hierarchical modeling techniques, including:

Adjacency List Model: In the adjacency list model, each record contains a reference to its parent record, allowing for efficient traversal of the hierarchy. This model is simple and flexible but can be inefficient for querying deeper hierarchies.

Nested Set Model: In the nested set model, each record is assigned a left and right value, indicating its position within the hierarchy. This model allows for efficient querying of hierarchical data but requires complex maintenance operations for updates and inserts.

Closure Table Model: In the closure table model, a separate table, known as a closure table, is used to store all possible paths between nodes in the hierarchy. This model offers efficient querying and flexible representation of hierarchical relationships but can be complex to implement and maintain.

CLI Command to Discuss Types of Hierarchical Modeling:
bashCopy code

$ discuss-hierarchical-modeling-types

3. Benefits of Hierarchical Modeling

Hierarchical modeling offers several benefits, including:

Clear representation of relationships: Hierarchical modeling provides a clear and intuitive representation of hierarchical relationships, making it easy to understand and navigate.

Efficient querying: Hierarchical models allow for efficient querying of hierarchical data, enabling fast retrieval of parent-child relationships and subtree operations.

Flexible structure: Hierarchical models are flexible and adaptable, allowing for dynamic changes to the hierarchy without significant structural modifications.

CLI Command to Highlight Benefits of Hierarchical Modeling:
bashCopy code

$ highlight-hierarchical-modeling-benefits

4. Practical Implementation Strategies

To implement hierarchical modeling effectively, consider the following strategies:

Choose the right model: Select the hierarchical modeling technique that best fits the requirements and characteristics of the data hierarchy.

Optimize for querying: Design the hierarchical model to optimize querying performance, considering factors such as indexing, caching, and query optimization techniques.

Handle updates and inserts carefully: Implement efficient algorithms and strategies for handling updates and inserts in hierarchical data structures to maintain data integrity and consistency.

CLI Command to Implement Hierarchical Modeling Strategies:

bashCopy code

```
$ implement-hierarchical-modeling-strategies
```

5. Common Challenges and Pitfalls

Despite its benefits, hierarchical modeling can also pose challenges and pitfalls:

Performance overhead: Hierarchical models may incur performance overhead, especially for deep or complex hierarchies, due to the need for recursive querying and traversal.

Maintenance complexity: Hierarchical models can be complex to maintain, especially when handling updates, inserts, and structural changes in the hierarchy.

Scalability limitations: Hierarchical models may face scalability limitations, particularly for large or dynamic hierarchies, requiring careful design and optimization to address scalability challenges.

CLI Command to Address Common Challenges:

bashCopy code

```
$ address-hierarchical-modeling-challenges
```

In summary, hierarchical modeling is a powerful technique for representing data relationships in a hierarchical structure. By understanding the different types of hierarchical modeling techniques, their benefits, implementation strategies, and common challenges, database designers can create efficient, scalable, and flexible hierarchical models that effectively capture and represent hierarchical relationships in their data.

Aggregation Design Considerations

Aggregation design is a crucial aspect of data warehousing, aimed at optimizing query performance by precalculating and storing aggregated data. This chapter explores various aggregation design considerations, including aggregation strategies, granularity, storage options, and practical implementation techniques.

CLI Command to Explore Aggregation Design Considerations:

bashCopy code

$ explore-aggregation-design-considerations

1. Understanding Aggregation Design

Aggregation design involves determining the appropriate level of data granularity for precalculating and storing aggregated data. Aggregates are summaries of detailed data, such as totals, averages, or counts, computed over a specific group of dimensions. By precalculating and storing aggregates, query performance can be significantly improved, especially for complex analytical queries involving large datasets.

CLI Command to Define Aggregation Design:

bashCopy code

$ define-aggregation-design

2. Granularity Considerations

Granularity refers to the level of detail at which data is stored and analyzed. Choosing the right granularity for aggregation design is crucial for balancing query performance with data accuracy and storage efficiency. Consider the following factors when determining granularity:

Business requirements: Align aggregation granularity with the analytical requirements of the business, ensuring that aggregated data provides meaningful insights for decision-making.

Query performance: Choose granularity levels that optimize query performance, reducing the need for expensive aggregate computations during query execution.

Storage efficiency: Balance granularity with storage efficiency, avoiding excessive storage overhead while ensuring that aggregated data retains sufficient detail for analysis.

CLI Command to Discuss Granularity Considerations:

bashCopy code

```
$ discuss-granularity-considerations
```

3. Aggregation Strategies

There are several aggregation strategies to consider when designing aggregates:

Full preaggregation: In full preaggregation, all possible combinations of dimensions and measures are precomputed and stored as aggregates. This approach offers maximum query performance but may require significant storage space.

Partial preaggregation: Partial preaggregation involves precomputing aggregates for selected dimensions or measures, optimizing query performance for specific analytical use cases while conserving storage space.

On-demand aggregation: On-demand aggregation calculates aggregates dynamically at query time, avoiding the need for precomputed aggregates but potentially resulting in slower query performance, especially for complex queries.

CLI Command to Discuss Aggregation Strategies:

bashCopy code

$ discuss-aggregation-strategies

4. Storage Options

When storing aggregated data, consider the following storage options:

Separate aggregate tables: Create separate tables to store precomputed aggregates, allowing for efficient querying and easy maintenance.

Materialized views: Use materialized views to store precomputed aggregates as virtual tables, providing the benefits of preaggregation without the need for additional storage space.

In-memory storage: Store aggregates in memory for fast access and query performance, leveraging in-memory databases or caching mechanisms to reduce query latency.

CLI Command to Explore Storage Options:

bashCopy code

$ explore-storage-options

5. Practical Implementation Techniques

To implement aggregation design effectively, consider the following techniques:

Identify key metrics: Identify the key performance metrics and analytical queries driving the aggregation design process, focusing on optimizing query performance for critical use cases.

Test and iterate: Test different aggregation designs and granularity levels using representative data and queries, iteratively refining the design based on performance benchmarks and user feedback.

Monitor and maintain: Monitor the performance of aggregated queries over time and adjust aggregation designs as data volumes and query patterns evolve, ensuring continued optimization and efficiency.

CLI Command to Implement Aggregation Design Techniques:

bashCopy code

```
$ implement-aggregation-design-techniques
```

In summary, aggregation design is a critical aspect of data warehousing, essential for optimizing query performance and enabling efficient analytical processing. By carefully considering factors such as granularity, aggregation strategies, storage options, and practical implementation techniques, data architects can design effective aggregation solutions that meet the analytical needs of their organization while maximizing query performance and storage efficiency.

Chapter 8: Data Modeling Tools and Software

Data modeling tools are essential for database designers and data architects to visualize, design, and manage the structure of their databases efficiently. This chapter explores some of the most popular data modeling tools available in the market, their features, benefits, and practical applications.

CLI Command to Explore Popular Data Modeling Tools:

bashCopy code

```
$ explore-popular-data-modeling-tools
```

1. Understanding Data Modeling Tools

Data modeling tools provide a graphical interface for creating and managing database schemas, allowing users to define tables, relationships, constraints, and other database objects visually. These tools typically support various data modeling notations, such as Entity-Relationship (ER) diagrams, UML diagrams, and dimensional models, making them versatile for different database design methodologies.

CLI Command to Define Data Modeling Tools:

bashCopy code

```
$ define-data-modeling-tools
```

2. Features and Capabilities

Popular data modeling tools offer a wide range of features and capabilities, including:

Visual design: Intuitive drag-and-drop interfaces for creating and modifying database objects, with support for customizable diagrams and layouts.

Reverse engineering: Ability to import existing database schemas from SQL scripts, database connections, or other sources, allowing users to visualize and analyze existing database structures.

Collaboration: Support for team collaboration features, such as version control, annotations, comments, and shared project repositories, enabling multiple users to work on the same database model simultaneously.

Code generation: Automatic generation of SQL DDL scripts or object-relational mapping (ORM) code from the data model, facilitating database schema deployment and application development.

Reporting and documentation: Built-in reporting and documentation features for generating comprehensive data model documentation, including entity descriptions, attribute definitions, relationships, and constraints.

CLI Command to Highlight Features of Data Modeling Tools:
bashCopy code

$ highlight-data-modeling-tool-features

3. Popular Data Modeling Tools

Some of the most popular data modeling tools in use today include:

ER/Studio: A comprehensive data modeling tool with support for various database platforms, advanced modeling features, and collaboration capabilities.

Toad Data Modeler: A user-friendly data modeling tool with support for both logical and physical modeling, reverse engineering, and extensive reporting options.

Microsoft Visio: Widely used for general diagramming purposes, Visio offers basic data modeling features, making it suitable for simple database design tasks.

Oracle SQL Developer Data Modeler: A free tool provided by Oracle for designing and managing Oracle databases, with support for both relational and dimensional modeling.

PowerDesigner: A robust data modeling and metadata management tool with support for enterprise architecture modeling, data lineage analysis, and integration with SAP systems.

CLI Command to List Popular Data Modeling Tools:

bashCopy code

$ list-popular-data-modeling-tools

4. Practical Applications

Data modeling tools find applications in various scenarios, including:

Database design: Creating and visualizing database schemas for new applications or database migrations.

Data governance: Establishing data standards, naming conventions, and data lineage documentation for regulatory compliance and data governance initiatives.

Business intelligence: Designing dimensional models for data warehouses and analytical systems, enabling efficient reporting and analysis.

Application development: Generating SQL DDL scripts or ORM code from data models for use in application development projects.

CLI Command to Discuss Practical Applications:

bashCopy code

$ discuss-data-modeling-tool-applications

5. Selection Considerations

When choosing a data modeling tool, consider the following factors:

Features and functionality: Evaluate the tool's features and capabilities based on your specific requirements, such as support for target database platforms, collaboration features, and reporting options.

Ease of use: Consider the tool's user interface and ease of use, ensuring that it meets the needs of both novice and experienced users.

Integration with existing tools and workflows: Ensure compatibility and integration with existing tools and workflows, such as database management systems, version control systems, and application development environments.

Cost and licensing: Consider the cost and licensing model of the tool, including upfront costs, subscription fees, and ongoing maintenance expenses.

CLI Command to Consider Selection Factors:

bashCopy code

$ consider-selection-factors

In summary, data modeling tools play a crucial role in database design and management, providing database designers and data architects with powerful features and capabilities for visualizing, designing, and documenting database schemas. By understanding the features, benefits, and practical applications of popular data modeling tools and considering factors such as functionality, ease of use, integration, and cost, organizations can select the right tool to meet their data modeling needs effectively.

Features and Comparison of Data Modeling Software

Data modeling software plays a pivotal role in the design and management of databases, offering a range of features to facilitate efficient schema creation, visualization, and maintenance. This chapter delves into the key features of data modeling software and provides a comparative analysis of popular tools available in the market.

CLI Command to Explore Features and Comparison:

bashCopy code

$ explore-data-modeling-software-features

1. Key Features of Data Modeling Software

Data modeling software typically offers a suite of features tailored to streamline the database design process. Some key features include:

Visual Design Interface: Intuitive drag-and-drop interfaces allow users to create and modify database objects graphically, facilitating rapid schema development.

Database Platform Support: Comprehensive support for various database management systems (DBMS), ensuring compatibility with popular platforms like Oracle, SQL Server, MySQL, and PostgreSQL.

Reverse Engineering: Capabilities to import existing database schemas from SQL scripts or live connections, enabling users to analyze and visualize current database structures.

Forward Engineering: Tools to generate SQL Data Definition Language (DDL) scripts from data models, automating the process of deploying schema changes to production environments.

Collaboration Features: Support for team collaboration, including version control, sharing of project repositories, and real-time collaboration on database models.

Documentation Generation: Built-in reporting and documentation features to generate comprehensive data model documentation, aiding in understanding and maintaining database structures.

Code Generation: Automated generation of object-relational mapping (ORM) code or data access layer code from data models, facilitating application development.

Data Validation: Validation checks to ensure data integrity and adherence to design constraints, helping to identify errors or inconsistencies in the database schema.

CLI Command to Highlight Key Features:

bashCopy code

$ highlight-data-modeling-software-features

2. Comparison of Popular Data Modeling Software

Several data modeling software options are available, each with its unique set of features and capabilities. Here's a comparison of some popular tools:

ER/Studio: Known for its robust feature set, ER/Studio offers comprehensive support for database platforms, advanced modeling features, and extensive collaboration capabilities.

Toad Data Modeler: User-friendly interface with support for both logical and physical modeling, reverse engineering, and customizable reporting options.

Microsoft Visio: Widely used for general diagramming purposes, Visio offers basic data modeling features suitable for simple database design tasks.

Oracle SQL Developer Data Modeler: Free tool provided by Oracle, featuring support for both relational and dimensional modeling, with integration with Oracle databases.

PowerDesigner: A comprehensive tool offering data modeling, metadata management, and enterprise architecture modeling, with integration capabilities with SAP systems.

CLI Command to Compare Data Modeling Software:
bashCopy code

```
$ compare-data-modeling-software
```

3. Factors to Consider in Comparison

When comparing data modeling software, consider the following factors:

Feature Set: Evaluate the range and depth of features offered by each tool, ensuring that it meets your specific requirements for database design and management.

Usability: Assess the user interface and ease of use, considering factors such as intuitiveness, navigation, and customization options.

Integration: Check compatibility and integration capabilities with existing tools and workflows, such as database management systems, version control systems, and application development environments.

Scalability: Consider the scalability of the software, ensuring that it can handle large and complex database models efficiently.

Cost: Evaluate the cost of licensing, subscription fees, and ongoing maintenance expenses, aligning with your budget and organizational requirements.

CLI Command to Consider Comparison Factors:

bashCopy code

```
$ consider-comparison-factors
```

In summary, data modeling software offers a range of features and capabilities to streamline the database design process, enabling users to create, visualize, and manage database schemas effectively. By comparing popular data modeling tools based on key features, usability, integration, scalability, and cost, organizations can make informed decisions in selecting the right tool to meet their database design needs and achieve their business objectives efficiently.

Chapter 9: Case Studies in Data Modeling for Warehousing

Data modeling is a crucial aspect of database design, allowing organizations to structure their data effectively to meet business requirements. Next, we explore real-world examples of data modeling, showcasing how different industries leverage data modeling techniques to address specific challenges and achieve their objectives.

CLI Command to Explore Real-world Data Modeling Examples:

bashCopy code

$ explore-real-world-data-modeling-examples

1. Retail Industry: Product Catalog Data Model

In the retail industry, managing product information efficiently is essential for inventory management, sales tracking, and customer engagement. A product catalog data model organizes product data into categories, attributes, and relationships, facilitating effective product management and analysis.

Example:

Entity: Product

Attributes: Name, Description, Price, Category

Relationships: Belongs to Category, Sold in Store, Purchased by Customer

CLI Command to Deploy Product Catalog Data Model:

bashCopy code

$ deploy-product-catalog-data-model

2. Healthcare Sector: Electronic Health Record (EHR) Data Model

Healthcare organizations deal with vast amounts of patient data, ranging from medical history and diagnoses to treatment plans and billing information. An electronic health record (EHR) data model structures patient data into standardized formats, enabling secure storage, retrieval, and analysis across healthcare systems.

Example:

Entity: Patient

Attributes: Name, Date of Birth, Gender, Medical History

Relationships: Visits Doctor, Receives Treatment, Pays Medical Bills

CLI Command to Deploy EHR Data Model:

bashCopy code

$ deploy-ehr-data-model

3. Financial Services: Banking Transaction Data Model

Financial institutions process millions of transactions daily, requiring robust data models to manage transactional data effectively. A banking transaction data model organizes transactional data into accounts, transactions, and related entities, enabling accurate financial reporting, fraud detection, and regulatory compliance.

Example:

Entity: Account

Attributes: Account Number, Balance, Owner

Relationships: Holds Funds, Initiates Transactions, Receives Deposits

CLI Command to Deploy Banking Transaction Data Model:

bashCopy code

$ deploy-banking-transaction-data-model

4. E-commerce: Customer Relationship Management (CRM) Data Model

E-commerce companies rely on customer data to personalize marketing campaigns, improve customer service, and drive sales. A customer relationship management (CRM) data model organizes customer data into profiles, interactions, and purchase history, enabling targeted marketing and customer retention efforts.

Example:

Entity: Customer

Attributes: Name, Email, Address, Purchase History

Relationships: Makes Purchase, Receives Marketing Emails, Contacts Customer Service

CLI Command to Deploy CRM Data Model:

bashCopy code

```
$ deploy-crm-data-model
```

5. Manufacturing Sector: Supply Chain Management (SCM) Data Model

Manufacturing companies manage complex supply chains involving suppliers, distributors, and production facilities. A supply chain management (SCM) data model structures supply chain data into entities such as suppliers, products, orders, and shipments, facilitating efficient inventory management, order fulfillment, and logistics planning.

Example:

Entity: Supplier

Attributes: Name, Contact Information, Products Supplied

Relationships: Supplies Materials, Receives Orders, Ships Products

CLI Command to Deploy SCM Data Model:

bashCopy code

```
$ deploy-scm-data-model
```

In summary, data modeling plays a crucial role in various industries, enabling organizations to structure their data effectively to support business operations, decision-making, and strategic initiatives. By exploring real-world examples of data modeling in industries such as retail, healthcare, finance, e-commerce, and manufacturing, organizations can gain insights into how data modeling techniques are applied to address specific challenges and achieve business objectives successfully.

Lessons Learned from Case Studies

Case studies provide invaluable insights into real-world applications of data modeling techniques and their impact on business outcomes. Next, we delve into several case studies from different industries, highlighting key lessons learned and best practices that can inform and guide future data modeling projects.

CLI Command to Explore Lessons Learned from Case Studies:

bashCopy code

$ explore-lessons-learned-from-case-studies

1. Retail Industry: Optimizing Product Recommendation Engines

Case Study: An online retail giant implemented a sophisticated product recommendation engine powered by data modeling techniques. By analyzing customer purchase history, browsing behavior, and demographic information, the retailer personalized product recommendations, resulting in a significant increase in sales and customer engagement.

Key Lesson: Utilize advanced data modeling techniques, such as collaborative filtering and machine learning algorithms, to drive personalized product recommendations and enhance customer satisfaction and retention.

2. Healthcare Sector: Enhancing Patient Care with Predictive Analytics

Case Study: A healthcare provider leveraged predictive analytics models built on data modeling principles to identify patients at high risk of developing chronic conditions. By analyzing electronic health record (EHR) data, the provider proactively intervened with preventive care measures, leading to improved patient outcomes and cost savings.

Key Lesson: Incorporate predictive analytics into data modeling efforts to anticipate future trends and risks, enabling proactive decision-making and resource allocation in healthcare settings.

3. Financial Services: Fraud Detection and Risk Management

Case Study: A banking institution implemented robust data modeling techniques to detect fraudulent transactions and mitigate financial risks. By analyzing transactional data patterns and customer behavior, the bank identified anomalous activities indicative of fraud, preventing potential losses and safeguarding customer assets.

Key Lesson: Implement data modeling solutions with built-in anomaly detection algorithms to identify and mitigate fraudulent activities effectively, ensuring financial security and regulatory compliance.

4. E-commerce: Improving Inventory Management and Demand Forecasting

Case Study: An e-commerce company utilized data modeling methodologies to optimize inventory management and demand forecasting processes. By analyzing historical sales data, seasonal trends, and market dynamics, the company accurately predicted product demand, minimizing stockouts and excess inventory costs.

Key Lesson: Leverage data modeling techniques, such as time series analysis and inventory optimization models, to optimize inventory management practices and improve supply chain efficiency in e-commerce operations.

5. Manufacturing Sector: Predictive Maintenance for Equipment Reliability

Case Study: A manufacturing plant implemented predictive maintenance models based on data modeling principles to improve equipment reliability and minimize downtime. By analyzing sensor data from production equipment, the plant proactively identified maintenance needs and scheduled repairs, reducing unplanned downtime and maximizing operational efficiency.

Key Lesson: Integrate predictive maintenance models into data modeling frameworks to enhance equipment reliability, optimize maintenance schedules, and prolong asset lifespan in manufacturing environments.

In summary, case studies offer valuable insights into the practical applications of data modeling techniques across various industries. By examining real-world examples of data modeling projects in retail, healthcare, finance, e-commerce, and manufacturing, organizations can glean valuable lessons and best practices for implementing data modeling initiatives effectively. From personalized product recommendations to predictive analytics for healthcare and fraud detection in finance, the lessons learned from these case studies underscore the transformative potential of data modeling in driving business success and innovation.

Chapter 10: Data Modeling Best Practices and Tips

Data modeling is a critical aspect of database design and management, laying the foundation for efficient data storage, retrieval, and analysis. Next, we explore best practices for effective data modeling, encompassing principles, techniques, and strategies to ensure the success of data modeling initiatives.

CLI Command to Explore Best Practices for Effective Data Modeling:

bashCopy code

```
$ explore-best-practices-data-modeling
```

1. Understand Business Requirements

Before embarking on a data modeling project, it's crucial to understand the business requirements and objectives thoroughly. Engage stakeholders from different departments to gather requirements, identify key data entities, relationships, and attributes, and prioritize data modeling efforts based on business value.

CLI Command to Gather Business Requirements:

bashCopy code

```
$ gather-business-requirements
```

2. Choose the Right Data Modeling Approach

Select the most appropriate data modeling approach based on the nature of the project and the requirements. Common approaches include Entity-Relationship (ER) modeling for relational databases, dimensional modeling for data warehouses, and graph modeling for complex relationships. Tailor the approach to align with the specific needs and characteristics of the data environment.

CLI Command to Choose Data Modeling Approach:

bashCopy code

```
$ choose-data-modeling-approach
```

3. Normalize Data Where Appropriate

Follow normalization principles to reduce redundancy and improve data integrity in relational databases. Break down data into atomic units and organize them into normalized forms, ensuring efficient storage and minimizing update anomalies. However, avoid over-normalization, which can lead to performance issues in certain scenarios.

CLI Command to Normalize Data:

bashCopy code

```
$ normalize-data
```

4. Denormalize for Performance Optimization

In situations where read performance is critical, consider denormalizing data to reduce join operations and improve query performance. Identify frequently accessed data entities and attributes and consolidate them into fewer tables, striking a balance between normalized and denormalized structures to optimize performance without sacrificing data integrity.

CLI Command to Denormalize Data:

bashCopy code

```
$ denormalize-data
```

5. Document Data Models Thoroughly

Comprehensive documentation is essential for understanding and maintaining data models over time. Document data entities, attributes, relationships, and constraints using standardized notations and tools. Include descriptions, data types, and business rules to provide context and clarity to stakeholders and future developers.

CLI Command to Document Data Models:

bashCopy code

```
$ document-data-models
```

6. Validate and Iterate

Validate data models through rigorous testing and review processes to identify errors, inconsistencies, and omissions. Conduct peer reviews, walkthroughs, and validation checks to ensure that data models accurately represent the business requirements. Iterate on the models based on feedback and evolving business needs.

CLI Command to Validate Data Models:

bashCopy code

$ validate-data-models

7. Implement Version Control

Implement version control practices to track changes, manage revisions, and maintain a history of data model iterations. Use version control systems such as Git to track model changes, collaborate with team members, and roll back to previous versions if needed. Ensure that changes are documented and communicated effectively.

CLI Command to Implement Version Control:

bashCopy code

$ implement-version-control

8. Foster Collaboration and Communication

Promote collaboration and communication among stakeholders, data modelers, developers, and business users throughout the data modeling process. Encourage open dialogue, feedback, and knowledge sharing to ensure alignment between data models and business objectives. Use collaborative tools and platforms to facilitate communication and collaboration.

CLI Command to Foster Collaboration:

bashCopy code

$ foster-collaboration-communication

9. Consider Performance and Scalability

Design data models with performance and scalability in mind to accommodate future growth and evolving requirements.

Optimize data structures, indexing strategies, and query patterns to ensure efficient data access and processing. Monitor performance metrics and scalability factors regularly and make adjustments as needed.

CLI Command to Monitor Performance:

bashCopy code

$ monitor-performance-scalability

10. Stay Abreast of Emerging Trends

Keep pace with emerging trends, technologies, and methodologies in data modeling to stay competitive and innovative. Stay informed about advancements in database systems, modeling tools, cloud computing, and big data analytics. Continuously evaluate and adapt data modeling practices to leverage the latest advancements and best practices.

CLI Command to Stay Abreast of Emerging Trends:

bashCopy code

$ stay-abreast-emerging-trends

In summary, effective data modeling requires a combination of best practices, methodologies, and collaborative efforts to align data structures with business requirements and objectives. By following these best practices, organizations can develop robust, scalable, and maintainable data models that serve as the foundation for successful data-driven initiatives. From understanding business requirements to fostering collaboration and staying abreast of emerging trends, adopting these practices can drive efficiency, accuracy, and innovation in data modeling endeavors.

Tips for Successful Data Modeling Implementation

Data modeling is a complex process that requires careful planning, execution, and management to ensure its success. Next, we discuss key tips and strategies for successfully implementing data modeling projects, covering various aspects from project planning to execution and maintenance.

CLI Command to Explore Tips for Successful Data Modeling Implementation:

bashCopy code

$ explore-tips-data-modeling-implementation

1. Define Clear Objectives and Scope

Before initiating a data modeling project, it's essential to define clear objectives and scope. Identify the specific business problems or opportunities that the data modeling initiative aims to address. Clearly outline the scope of the project, including the data sources, entities, relationships, and outcomes expected.

CLI Command to Define Objectives and Scope:

bashCopy code

$ define-objectives-scope

2. Establish a Cross-functional Team

Assemble a cross-functional team with diverse expertise and perspectives to drive the data modeling project forward. Include representatives from business units, IT departments, data analysts, and end-users to ensure alignment with business goals and requirements. Foster collaboration and communication among team members throughout the project lifecycle.

CLI Command to Establish Cross-functional Team:

bashCopy code

$ establish-cross-functional-team

3. Conduct Thorough Data Profiling and Analysis

Before designing data models, conduct thorough data profiling and analysis to understand the characteristics, quality, and relationships of the underlying data. Identify data sources, assess data quality, and analyze data patterns and distributions to inform data modeling decisions. Use data profiling tools and techniques to gain insights into the data landscape.

CLI Command to Conduct Data Profiling:

bashCopy code

```
$ conduct-data-profiling-analysis
```

4. Leverage Agile Methodologies

Adopt agile methodologies such as Scrum or Kanban to manage data modeling projects iteratively and adaptively. Break down the project into smaller, manageable tasks or sprints, and prioritize deliverables based on business value and feedback. Conduct regular sprint reviews and retrospectives to evaluate progress and make adjustments as needed.

CLI Command to Leverage Agile Methodologies:

bashCopy code

```
$ leverage-agile-methodologies
```

5. Use Visual Modeling Tools

Utilize visual modeling tools and software to design, document, and communicate data models effectively. Choose tools that support industry-standard notations such as Entity-Relationship (ER) diagrams, UML diagrams, and dimensional models. Visualize complex relationships, hierarchies, and structures to facilitate understanding and collaboration among stakeholders.

CLI Command to Use Visual Modeling Tools:

bashCopy code

```
$ use-visual-modeling-tools
```

6. Implement Data Governance Policies

Establish data governance policies and frameworks to ensure the quality, integrity, and security of data assets throughout their lifecycle. Define standards, policies, and procedures for data modeling, metadata management, data quality, and access control. Implement data governance tools and workflows to enforce compliance and accountability.

CLI Command to Implement Data Governance Policies:

bashCopy code

$ implement-data-governance-policies

7. Prioritize Data Quality and Consistency

Emphasize data quality and consistency as core principles of data modeling implementation. Define data quality metrics and standards, such as accuracy, completeness, consistency, and timeliness, and incorporate them into data modeling processes. Implement data validation rules, constraints, and automated checks to maintain data integrity and reliability.

CLI Command to Prioritize Data Quality:

bashCopy code

$ prioritize-data-quality-consistency

8. Foster Collaboration and Communication

Promote collaboration and communication among stakeholders, data modelers, and end-users throughout the data modeling project. Conduct regular meetings, workshops, and presentations to share progress, gather feedback, and address concerns. Encourage open dialogue and knowledge sharing to ensure alignment and transparency across all parties involved.

CLI Command to Foster Collaboration:

bashCopy code

$ foster-collaboration-communication

9. Invest in Training and Education

Provide training and education opportunities for team members to enhance their skills and knowledge in data modeling techniques and tools. Offer workshops, seminars, and certifications on data modeling best practices, methodologies, and technologies. Invest in continuous learning and development to empower the team to excel in their roles.

CLI Command to Invest in Training:

bashCopy code

$ invest-training-education

10. Monitor and Measure Success Metrics

Establish key performance indicators (KPIs) and success metrics to monitor the effectiveness and impact of data modeling initiatives. Track metrics such as project timelines, data quality improvements, stakeholder satisfaction, and business outcomes achieved. Regularly assess progress against predefined KPIs and adjust strategies accordingly.

CLI Command to Monitor Success Metrics:

bashCopy code

$ monitor-measure-success-metrics

In summary, successful data modeling implementation requires careful planning, execution, and management across various stages of the project lifecycle. By following these tips and strategies, organizations can maximize the effectiveness and value of their data modeling initiatives, driving business innovation, agility, and competitiveness. From defining clear objectives to fostering collaboration and prioritizing data quality, adopting these best practices can lead to successful outcomes and lasting impact in data-driven organizations.

BOOK 3
ADVANCED ETL TECHNIQUES FOR DATA WAREHOUSING OPTIMIZATION

ROB BOTWRIGHT

Chapter 1: Introduction to ETL (Extract, Transform, Load) Processes

ETL (Extract, Transform, Load) processes are fundamental to data warehousing, enabling organizations to extract data from multiple sources, transform it into a consistent format, and load it into a centralized data repository for analysis and reporting. Next, we provide an in-depth overview of ETL processes, covering their components, methodologies, and best practices.

CLI Command to Explore Overview of ETL Processes:

bashCopy code

```
$ explore-etl-processes-overview
```

1. Extracting Data

The first step in the ETL process is extracting data from various sources such as databases, files, APIs, and streaming platforms. Organizations may use different extraction methods depending on the source systems and data formats. Common extraction techniques include full extraction, incremental extraction, and change data capture (CDC).

CLI Command to Extract Data:

bashCopy code

```
$ extract-data
```

2. Transforming Data

After extracting data, the next step is transforming it into a consistent format suitable for analysis and storage. Data transformation involves cleaning, validating, enriching, and restructuring data to meet business requirements and standards. Transformations may include data cleansing, aggregation, filtering, and joining multiple datasets.

CLI Command to Transform Data:

bashCopy code

$ transform-data

3. Loading Data

Once data is transformed, it is loaded into the target data warehouse or data mart for storage and analysis. Loading data involves inserting, updating, or appending records to the destination tables in the data repository. Organizations may employ different loading techniques such as bulk loading, incremental loading, or real-time streaming based on their requirements.

CLI Command to Load Data:

bashCopy code

$ load-data

4. ETL Methodologies

Several methodologies guide the design and implementation of ETL processes, including batch processing, trickle loading, and real-time data integration. Batch processing involves processing data in predefined batches at scheduled intervals, while trickle loading processes data continuously in small increments. Real-time data integration enables immediate processing and delivery of data as it becomes available.

CLI Command to Choose ETL Methodologies:

bashCopy code

$ choose-etl-methodologies

5. Best Practices for ETL Processes

Effective ETL processes rely on best practices to ensure efficiency, reliability, and scalability. Some best practices include data profiling to understand data quality and structure, error handling to manage exceptions and failures gracefully, and metadata management to document and track data lineage. Additionally, organizations should prioritize performance optimization, data security, and compliance with regulatory requirements.

CLI Command to Implement Best Practices:

bashCopy code

$ implement-best-practices-etl

6. Tools and Technologies

A variety of tools and technologies support ETL processes, ranging from open-source frameworks like Apache Hadoop and Apache Spark to commercial ETL platforms such as Informatica, Talend, and IBM DataStage. These tools offer features for data integration, transformation, scheduling, monitoring, and management, empowering organizations to streamline and automate their ETL workflows.

CLI Command to Explore ETL Tools and Technologies:

bashCopy code

$ explore-etl-tools-technologies

7. ETL Workflow Management

Managing ETL workflows involves orchestrating and monitoring the entire ETL process from data extraction to loading. Organizations use workflow management tools and platforms to design, schedule, execute, and monitor ETL workflows efficiently. These tools provide features for workflow automation, dependency management, error handling, and performance optimization.

CLI Command to Manage ETL Workflows:

bashCopy code

$ manage-etl-workflows

8. Scalability and Performance Optimization

Scalability and performance optimization are critical considerations in ETL processes, especially in large-scale data integration environments. Organizations should design ETL architectures that can scale horizontally and vertically to handle increasing data volumes and processing loads. Techniques such as parallel processing, distributed computing, and caching can improve performance and throughput.

CLI Command to Optimize ETL Performance:

bashCopy code

$ optimize-etl-performance

9. Data Quality Assurance

Ensuring data quality is essential for the success of ETL processes and downstream analytics. Organizations should implement data quality checks, validations, and profiling techniques to identify and rectify inconsistencies, errors, and anomalies in the data. Data quality tools and frameworks help automate data validation, cleansing, and enrichment tasks to maintain high data quality standards.

CLI Command to Assure Data Quality:

bashCopy code

$ assure-data-quality

10. Monitoring and Maintenance

Continuous monitoring and maintenance are essential to ensure the reliability and integrity of ETL processes over time. Organizations should establish monitoring dashboards, alerts, and performance metrics to track ETL job execution, data accuracy, and system health. Regular maintenance activities include job scheduling, error handling, log analysis, and version control.

CLI Command to Monitor and Maintain ETL Processes:

bashCopy code

```
$ monitor-maintain-etl
```

In summary, ETL processes play a crucial role in data warehousing and analytics, enabling organizations to extract, transform, and load data from diverse sources into centralized repositories for analysis and reporting. By following best practices, leveraging appropriate methodologies and tools, and prioritizing scalability, performance, and data quality, organizations can build robust and efficient ETL workflows that drive data-driven decision-making and business success.

Importance of ETL in Data Warehousing

ETL (Extract, Transform, Load) processes play a pivotal role in data warehousing by facilitating the movement and transformation of data from diverse sources into a structured format suitable for analysis and reporting. Next, we delve into the significance of ETL in data warehousing, highlighting its key benefits, challenges, and best practices.

CLI Command to Explore the Importance of ETL in Data Warehousing:

bashCopy code

```
$ explore-importance-etl-data-warehousing
```

1. Data Integration

One of the primary roles of ETL in data warehousing is data integration. Organizations often have data scattered across multiple sources, including databases, files, applications, and cloud services. ETL processes enable the seamless integration of data from disparate sources into a centralized data warehouse, providing a unified view of the organization's data assets.

CLI Command to Integrate Data:

bashCopy code

$ integrate-data

2. Data Cleansing and Standardization

Data quality is critical for accurate analysis and decision-making. ETL processes include data cleansing and standardization steps to identify and rectify inconsistencies, errors, and duplicates in the data. By cleansing and standardizing data during the transformation phase, organizations ensure that only high-quality, reliable data is loaded into the data warehouse.

CLI Command to Cleanse and Standardize Data:

bashCopy code

$ cleanse-standardize-data

3. Data Transformation

ETL processes transform raw data into a structured format that is optimized for analysis and reporting. Transformation tasks may include data aggregation, normalization, denormalization, and enrichment. Through these transformations, organizations can derive insights, identify trends, and make informed decisions based on the data stored in the data warehouse.

CLI Command to Transform Data:

bashCopy code

$ transform-data

4. Historical Data Analysis

Data warehousing allows organizations to store historical data over time, enabling retrospective analysis and trend identification. ETL processes play a crucial role in loading historical data into the data warehouse and maintaining its integrity. By storing historical data, organizations can analyze past performance, track trends, and forecast future outcomes more effectively.

CLI Command to Analyze Historical Data:

bashCopy code

$ analyze-historical-data

5. Real-time Data Processing

In addition to historical data analysis, ETL processes can also support real-time or near-real-time data processing. Organizations can implement streaming ETL pipelines to ingest, process, and analyze data in real-time as it becomes available. Real-time data processing enables faster insights, immediate decision-making, and responsiveness to changing business conditions.

CLI Command to Implement Real-time Data Processing:

bashCopy code

$ implement-real-time-processing

6. Decision Support and Business Intelligence

Data warehousing serves as the foundation for decision support and business intelligence (BI) initiatives within organizations. By centralizing and organizing data in a data warehouse, organizations empower decision-makers with access to timely, accurate, and actionable insights. ETL processes ensure that data is transformed and loaded efficiently to support BI applications and analytics dashboards.

CLI Command to Support Decision Support and BI:

bashCopy code

$ support-decision-support-bi

7. Regulatory Compliance

Many industries are subject to regulatory requirements regarding data storage, security, and privacy. ETL processes help organizations comply with regulatory standards by ensuring the accuracy, integrity, and security of data stored in the data warehouse. By implementing data governance and access control measures within ETL workflows, organizations can maintain compliance with relevant regulations.

CLI Command to Ensure Regulatory Compliance:

bashCopy code

```
$ ensure-regulatory-compliance
```

8. Scalability and Performance

As organizations grow and data volumes increase, scalability and performance become crucial considerations in data warehousing. ETL processes should be designed to scale horizontally and vertically to accommodate growing data volumes and processing loads. Techniques such as parallel processing, distributed computing, and optimization are employed to enhance ETL scalability and performance.

CLI Command to Ensure Scalability and Performance:

bashCopy code

```
$ ensure-scalability-performance
```

9. Data Governance and Security

Data governance and security are paramount in data warehousing to protect sensitive information and ensure data quality and integrity. ETL processes incorporate data governance policies, access controls, and encryption mechanisms to safeguard data throughout its lifecycle. By enforcing security measures within ETL workflows, organizations mitigate the risk of data breaches and unauthorized access.

CLI Command to Implement Data Governance and Security:

bashCopy code

$ implement-data-governance-security

10. Cost Efficiency

Effective ETL processes contribute to cost efficiency by streamlining data integration, transformation, and loading tasks. By automating repetitive tasks and optimizing resource utilization, organizations can reduce operational costs associated with data warehousing. ETL tools and platforms offer features for workflow automation, scheduling, and resource management, further enhancing cost efficiency.

CLI Command to Ensure Cost Efficiency:

bashCopy code

$ ensure-cost-efficiency

In summary, ETL processes are indispensable in data warehousing, enabling organizations to integrate, transform, and load data from diverse sources into a centralized repository for analysis and reporting. By leveraging ETL processes effectively, organizations can improve data quality, enhance decision-making, ensure compliance, and drive business success in today's data-driven world.

Chapter 2: Data Extraction Strategies and Tools

Data extraction is the first step in the ETL (Extract, Transform, Load) process, where data is extracted from various sources such as databases, files, APIs, and web services. Next, we explore different methods of data extraction, their advantages, challenges, and best practices.

CLI Command to Explore Methods of Data Extraction:

bashCopy code

```
$ explore-data-extraction-methods
```

1. Full Extraction

Full extraction, also known as full load, involves extracting all the data from the source system each time the extraction process runs. This method is straightforward and suitable for small datasets or when the source data changes infrequently. However, full extraction can be time-consuming and resource-intensive, especially for large datasets.

CLI Command for Full Extraction:

bashCopy code

```
$ full-extraction
```

2. Incremental Extraction

Incremental extraction involves extracting only the data that has changed since the last extraction. This method is more efficient than full extraction as it reduces the amount of data transferred and processed during each extraction run. Incremental extraction typically relies on timestamps, sequence numbers, or change data capture (CDC) mechanisms to identify and extract only the delta changes.

CLI Command for Incremental Extraction:
bashCopy code

$ incremental-extraction

3. Change Data Capture (CDC)

Change Data Capture (CDC) is a technique used to identify and capture changes made to source data since the last extraction. CDC mechanisms track inserts, updates, and deletes in the source system's data records and capture these changes for extraction. CDC enables real-time or near-real-time data integration by capturing changes as they occur, minimizing latency and ensuring data freshness.

CLI Command for Change Data Capture:
bashCopy code

$ cdc-extraction

4. Database Query

Database query extraction involves executing SQL queries against the source database to retrieve data. This method allows for selective extraction based on specific criteria, such as date ranges, filters, and joins. Database query extraction is efficient for extracting large volumes of data from relational databases and provides flexibility in data selection and transformation.

CLI Command for Database Query Extraction:
bashCopy code

$ database-query-extraction

5. API-Based Extraction

API-based extraction involves interfacing with application programming interfaces (APIs) provided by source systems to retrieve data programmatically. Many modern applications expose APIs that allow developers to access data in a structured format. API-based extraction is suitable for extracting data from web services, cloud platforms, and SaaS applications and supports authentication, pagination, and rate limiting.

CLI Command for API-Based Extraction:

bashCopy code

$ api-based-extraction

6. File-Based Extraction

File-based extraction involves extracting data from files stored in various formats such as CSV, Excel, JSON, XML, and text files. This method is commonly used for batch processing and data interchange between systems. File-based extraction supports reading files from local file systems, network shares, FTP servers, and cloud storage services.

CLI Command for File-Based Extraction:

bashCopy code

$ file-based-extraction

7. Web Scraping

Web scraping is a technique used to extract data from websites and web pages. It involves parsing HTML or XML documents to extract specific data elements based on predefined patterns or rules. Web scraping is often used for extracting structured data from online sources such as news articles, product listings, and social media posts.

CLI Command for Web Scraping:

bashCopy code

$ web-scraping-extraction

8. Streaming Data Extraction

Streaming data extraction involves capturing and processing real-time data streams from sources such as sensors, IoT devices, social media feeds, and financial markets. This method enables organizations to ingest and analyze streaming data for immediate insights and decision-making. Streaming data extraction often requires specialized tools and platforms capable of handling high-volume, high-velocity data streams.

CLI Command for Streaming Data Extraction:

bashCopy code

```
$ streaming-data-extraction
```

9. Cloud Data Integration

Cloud data integration platforms offer built-in capabilities for extracting data from cloud-based sources such as databases, data warehouses, SaaS applications, and cloud storage services. These platforms provide connectors, APIs, and data pipelines for seamless integration and extraction of data from various cloud environments. Cloud data integration simplifies the process of extracting and loading data into cloud-based data warehouses and analytics platforms.

CLI Command for Cloud Data Integration:

bashCopy code

```
$ cloud-data-extraction
```

10. Best Practices for Data Extraction

Effective data extraction requires adherence to best practices to ensure efficiency, reliability, and scalability. Some best practices include data profiling to understand source data characteristics, data validation to ensure data integrity, error handling to manage exceptions gracefully, and performance optimization to minimize extraction latency. Additionally, organizations should prioritize data security, compliance, and documentation throughout the data extraction process.

CLI Command for Implementing Best Practices:

bashCopy code

```
$ implement-best-practices-data-extraction
```

In summary, data extraction is a critical component of the ETL process, enabling organizations to extract data from diverse sources and prepare it for analysis and reporting in data warehouses and analytics platforms. By leveraging various extraction methods, organizations can efficiently ingest data from databases, files, APIs, web services, and streaming sources, driving data-driven decision-making and business success.

Comparison of Data Extraction Tools
In the realm of data extraction, there exists a plethora of tools designed to facilitate the extraction of data from diverse sources such as databases, files, APIs, and web services. Each tool comes with its own set of features, strengths, and limitations. Next, we will conduct a comprehensive comparison of popular data extraction tools, evaluating their functionality, scalability, ease of use, and suitability for different use cases.

CLI Command to Explore Data Extraction Tools Comparison:
bashCopy code
```
$ explore-data-extraction-tools-comparison
```

1. Apache NiFi
Apache NiFi is a powerful data integration platform that provides a visual interface for designing data flows and automating data movement tasks. It offers a wide range of connectors and processors for extracting, transforming, and loading data. NiFi's drag-and-drop interface simplifies the development of data pipelines, making it suitable for both simple and complex data extraction requirements.

CLI Command for Apache NiFi:
bashCopy code
$ use-apache-nifi

2. Talend Open Studio

Talend Open Studio is an open-source data integration tool that offers a comprehensive set of features for data extraction, transformation, and loading (ETL). It provides a graphical interface for designing ETL workflows and supports a wide range of connectors for extracting data from various sources. Talend's code generation capabilities enable developers to deploy ETL jobs as standalone applications or integrate them into existing systems.

CLI Command for Talend Open Studio:
bashCopy code
$ use-talend-open-studio

3. Informatica PowerCenter

Informatica PowerCenter is a leading enterprise data integration platform known for its scalability, performance, and robust feature set. It offers a visual development environment for designing ETL workflows and supports high-volume data extraction from heterogeneous sources. PowerCenter's advanced transformation capabilities and built-in data quality features make it suitable for complex data extraction and integration scenarios.

CLI Command for Informatica PowerCenter:
bashCopy code
$ use-informatica-powercenter

4. Microsoft SQL Server Integration Services (SSIS)

Microsoft SQL Server Integration Services (SSIS) is a powerful ETL tool included with Microsoft SQL Server. It provides a visual development environment for building data integration solutions and offers a rich set of built-in components for data extraction, transformation, and loading. SSIS integrates seamlessly with other Microsoft products and services, making it an ideal choice for organizations with existing Microsoft infrastructure.

CLI Command for SSIS:

bashCopy code

$ use-ssis

5. Pentaho Data Integration (Kettle)

Pentaho Data Integration, also known as Kettle, is an open-source ETL tool that offers a robust set of features for data extraction, transformation, and loading. It provides a graphical user interface for designing ETL jobs and supports a wide range of data sources and formats. Pentaho's extensible architecture and community-driven development make it a popular choice for organizations seeking cost-effective data integration solutions.

CLI Command for Pentaho Data Integration:

bashCopy code

$ use-pentaho-data-integration

6. Apache Spark

Apache Spark is a distributed computing framework that offers built-in support for data extraction, transformation, and analysis. It provides a unified API for working with various data sources, including files, databases, and streaming data. Spark's in-memory processing capabilities enable fast and scalable data extraction, making it suitable for big data and real-time analytics applications.

CLI Command for Apache Spark:

bashCopy code

$ use-apache-spark

7. Amazon Glue

Amazon Glue is a fully managed ETL service provided by Amazon Web Services (AWS). It offers a serverless architecture for running ETL jobs at scale without provisioning or managing infrastructure. Glue provides a visual interface for designing ETL workflows and supports automatic schema discovery, data cataloging, and job scheduling. With its pay-as-you-go pricing model, Glue is well-suited for cloud-based data extraction and integration.

CLI Command for Amazon Glue:

bashCopy code

```
$ use-amazon-glue
```

8. Google Cloud Dataflow

Google Cloud Dataflow is a fully managed stream and batch processing service provided by Google Cloud Platform (GCP). It offers a unified programming model for building data processing pipelines and supports data extraction from various sources, including Google Cloud Storage, BigQuery, and external systems. Dataflow's autoscaling capabilities and integration with other GCP services make it a preferred choice for data extraction and processing in the cloud.

CLI Command for Google Cloud Dataflow:

bashCopy code

```
$ use-google-cloud-dataflow
```

9. IBM DataStage

IBM DataStage is an enterprise-grade ETL tool known for its scalability, reliability, and performance. It provides a visual development environment for designing and deploying ETL jobs and offers a wide range of connectors for data extraction from diverse sources. DataStage's parallel processing capabilities and job orchestration features make it suitable for large-scale data integration projects in complex environments.

CLI Command for IBM DataStage:

bashCopy code

$ use-ibm-datastage

10. Apache Sqoop

Apache Sqoop is a command-line tool designed for efficiently transferring data between Apache Hadoop and relational databases. It supports incremental data extraction and parallel data loading, making it well-suited for large-scale data migration and integration tasks. Sqoop integrates seamlessly with Hadoop ecosystem components such as HDFS, Hive, and HBase, enabling organizations to leverage their existing infrastructure for data extraction and processing.

CLI Command for Apache Sqoop:

bashCopy code

$ use-apache-sqoop

In summary, the choice of data extraction tool depends on factors such as the complexity of data sources, scalability requirements, integration capabilities, and budget constraints. By carefully evaluating the features and capabilities of different data extraction tools, organizations can select the most suitable tool for their specific use cases and achieve efficient and reliable data integration across their enterprise.

Chapter 3: Transforming Data: Cleaning, Enriching, and Standardizing

Data cleaning, also known as data cleansing or data scrubbing, is a crucial step in the data preparation process. It involves identifying and correcting errors, inconsistencies, and inaccuracies in datasets to ensure data quality and reliability for analysis and decision-making. Next, we explore various techniques for cleaning data and discuss the challenges associated with this critical task.

CLI Command to Explore Data Cleaning Techniques:

bashCopy code

```
$ explore-data-cleaning-techniques
```

1. Data Profiling

Data profiling is the first step in the data cleaning process, where analysts examine the structure, quality, and content of datasets to identify potential issues. Data profiling tools analyze data distributions, patterns, and anomalies to uncover missing values, duplicates, outliers, and other inconsistencies. By gaining insights into the characteristics of the data, analysts can develop effective cleaning strategies to address identified issues.

CLI Command for Data Profiling:

bashCopy code

```
$ data-profiling
```

2. Handling Missing Values

Missing values are a common challenge in datasets and can adversely affect the accuracy and reliability of analysis results. Techniques for handling missing values include imputation, where missing values are replaced with estimated or calculated values based on statistical methods such as mean, median, or mode. Another approach is to remove rows or columns with missing values, although this may result in loss of valuable data.

CLI Command for Handling Missing Values:

bashCopy code

$ handle-missing-values

3. Data Standardization

Data standardization involves converting data into a uniform format or representation to facilitate consistency and comparability across datasets. This may include converting categorical variables to a common format, normalizing numerical values, and applying standard units of measurement. Standardization ensures that data is consistent and compatible for analysis and reduces the risk of errors and misinterpretation.

CLI Command for Data Standardization:

bashCopy code

$ data-standardization

4. Removing Duplicates

Duplicate records in datasets can skew analysis results and lead to inaccurate conclusions. Identifying and removing duplicate records is essential for maintaining data quality. Techniques for removing duplicates include deduplication, where identical records are identified and eliminated based on specified criteria such as key fields or combinations of attributes. Deduplication ensures that each record in the dataset is unique and representative.

CLI Command for Removing Duplicates:

bashCopy code

$ remove-duplicates

5. Correcting Inaccurate Data

Inaccurate data, such as typos, misspellings, and erroneous values, can compromise the integrity of datasets. Techniques for correcting inaccurate data include data validation, where data is checked against predefined rules or constraints to identify discrepancies. Data cleaning tools may also employ fuzzy matching algorithms to identify and correct spelling variations or inconsistencies in textual data.

CLI Command for Correcting Inaccurate Data:

bashCopy code

$ correct-inaccurate-data

6. Handling Outliers

Outliers are data points that deviate significantly from the rest of the dataset and may indicate errors or anomalies. Techniques for handling outliers include statistical methods such as z-score normalization, where outliers are identified based on their deviation from the mean or median of the dataset. Outliers can be removed, transformed, or treated separately depending on their impact on analysis objectives.

CLI Command for Handling Outliers:

bashCopy code

$ handle-outliers

7. Data Transformation

Data transformation involves converting data from one format or structure to another to meet analysis requirements. Techniques for data transformation include scaling, where numerical values are normalized to a common range, and encoding, where categorical variables are converted into numerical representations. Data transformation ensures that data is appropriately formatted and prepared for analysis tasks.

CLI Command for Data Transformation:

bashCopy code

$ data-transformation

8. Dealing with Inconsistent Formats

Inconsistent data formats, such as date formats, currency symbols, and units of measurement, can pose challenges for data analysis and integration. Techniques for dealing with inconsistent formats include data parsing and formatting, where data is parsed into standardized formats using regular expressions or parsing libraries. Data normalization techniques may also be employed to ensure consistent representation of data across datasets.

CLI Command for Dealing with Inconsistent Formats:

bashCopy code

$ deal-with-inconsistent-formats

9. Addressing Data Quality Issues

Data quality issues encompass a range of challenges, including accuracy, completeness, consistency, and timeliness of data. Techniques for addressing data quality issues include data cleansing, where errors and inconsistencies are corrected or removed, and data enrichment, where missing or incomplete data is supplemented with additional information from external sources. Data quality monitoring and reporting mechanisms are essential for ensuring ongoing data quality management.

CLI Command for Addressing Data Quality Issues:

bashCopy code

$ address-data-quality-issues

10. Challenges in Data Cleaning

Despite the importance of data cleaning, several challenges exist in the process. These challenges include scalability, as large datasets may require significant computational resources and processing time for cleaning tasks. Data cleaning also requires domain expertise and knowledge of the underlying data semantics, making it essential to involve subject matter experts in the process. Additionally, data privacy and security concerns may arise when handling sensitive or confidential information during the cleaning process.

CLI Command for Identifying Data Cleaning Challenges:
bashCopy code

$ identify-data-cleaning-challenges

In summary, data cleaning is a critical step in the data preparation process, ensuring that datasets are accurate, reliable, and suitable for analysis and decision-making. By employing a combination of techniques such as data profiling, handling missing values, standardization, and outlier detection, organizations can enhance the quality and integrity of their data assets. Despite the challenges involved, effective data cleaning practices are essential for deriving meaningful insights and driving business success.

Data enrichment is the process of enhancing raw datasets with additional information to improve their quality, accuracy, and value for analysis and decision-making. Next, we explore various strategies and techniques for enriching data, including data augmentation, entity resolution, and external data integration.

CLI Command to Explore Data Enrichment Strategies:
bashCopy code

$ explore-data-enrichment-strategies

1. Data Augmentation

Data augmentation involves adding new features or attributes to existing datasets to provide additional context or insights. This can include enriching datasets with demographic information, geographic data, or behavioral data obtained from external sources. For example, appending demographic attributes such as age, gender, or income level to customer datasets can provide valuable insights for segmentation and targeting in marketing campaigns.

CLI Command for Data Augmentation:

bashCopy code

$ data-augmentation

2. Entity Resolution

Entity resolution, also known as record linkage or deduplication, is the process of identifying and merging duplicate or related records within datasets. This involves comparing records based on common attributes such as names, addresses, or unique identifiers and resolving conflicts to create a single, unified view of entities. Entity resolution techniques may employ probabilistic matching algorithms, fuzzy matching techniques, or machine learning models to achieve accurate and efficient record linkage.

CLI Command for Entity Resolution:

bashCopy code

$ entity-resolution

3. External Data Integration

External data integration involves integrating additional data from external sources into existing datasets to enrich their content and expand their scope. This can include incorporating data from third-party sources such as government databases, industry reports, social media feeds, or public APIs. For example, integrating weather data into sales datasets can provide insights into the impact of weather conditions on consumer behavior and purchasing patterns.

CLI Command for External Data Integration:
bashCopy code

```
$ external-data-integration
```

4. Textual Analysis and Natural Language Processing (NLP)

Textual analysis and natural language processing (NLP) techniques can be used to extract valuable information from unstructured text data and enrich datasets with semantic meaning. This may involve sentiment analysis, entity recognition, topic modeling, or named entity recognition to extract entities, relationships, and sentiment from textual data sources such as customer reviews, social media posts, or news articles.

CLI Command for Textual Analysis and NLP:
bashCopy code

```
$ textual-analysis-nlp
```

5. Geospatial Data Integration

Geospatial data integration involves incorporating geographic information into datasets to enable spatial analysis and visualization. This can include enriching datasets with latitude and longitude coordinates, geocoding addresses, or integrating spatial boundaries such as postal codes, administrative regions, or geographic features. Geospatial data enrichment enables organizations to analyze spatial relationships, proximity, and distribution patterns in their data.

CLI Command for Geospatial Data Integration:
bashCopy code

```
$ geospatial-data-integration
```

6. Social Network Analysis (SNA)

Social network analysis (SNA) techniques can be used to enrich datasets with network attributes and relationships, such as connections, influence, and centrality measures. This may involve analyzing social media data to identify communities, influencers, or patterns of interaction among users. By enriching datasets with social network attributes, organizations can gain insights into social dynamics, information diffusion, and influence propagation in their networks.

CLI Command for Social Network Analysis:

bashCopy code

```
$ social-network-analysis
```

7. Time-Series Analysis

Time-series analysis involves analyzing sequential data points collected over time to identify patterns, trends, and anomalies. Enriching datasets with time-series attributes such as timestamps, date ranges, or periodicity indicators enables organizations to perform temporal analysis and forecasting. Time-series enrichment techniques may involve aggregating data into meaningful time intervals, detecting seasonality, or identifying temporal dependencies and correlations.

CLI Command for Time-Series Analysis:

bashCopy code

```
$ time-series-analysis
```

8. Machine Learning and Predictive Modeling

Machine learning and predictive modeling techniques can be used to enrich datasets with predictive insights and actionable recommendations. This may involve training machine learning models on historical data to predict future outcomes, classify data into categories, or identify patterns and relationships. By enriching datasets with predictive attributes, organizations can make data-driven decisions and anticipate future trends and events.

CLI Command for Machine Learning and Predictive Modeling:

bashCopy code

```
$ machine-learning-predictive-modeling
```

9. Data Visualization and Exploration

Data visualization and exploration techniques can be used to enrich datasets with visual representations and interactive dashboards. This may involve creating charts, graphs, maps, or other visualizations to illustrate patterns, trends, and relationships in the data. By enriching datasets with visualizations, organizations can communicate insights more effectively and facilitate data-driven decision-making.

CLI Command for Data Visualization and Exploration:

bashCopy code

```
$ data-visualization-exploration
```

10. Quality Assurance and Validation

Quality assurance and validation processes are essential for ensuring the accuracy, reliability, and consistency of enriched datasets. This may involve performing data validation checks, error detection, and outlier detection to identify and correct errors or inconsistencies in the data. Quality assurance techniques may also include data profiling, metadata management, and documentation to ensure that enriched datasets meet quality standards and comply with regulatory requirements.

CLI Command for Quality Assurance and Validation:

bashCopy code

$ quality-assurance-validation

In summary, data enrichment plays a vital role in enhancing the value and utility of datasets for analysis and decision-making. By employing a combination of strategies and techniques such as data augmentation, entity resolution, external data integration, and advanced analytics, organizations can enrich their datasets with additional information and insights. Effective data enrichment enables organizations to unlock the full potential of their data assets and derive actionable insights to drive business success.

Chapter 4: Advanced Data Transformation Techniques

Data transformation is a crucial step in the data processing pipeline, where raw data is manipulated and converted into a format suitable for analysis, reporting, and decision-making. While basic transformation techniques such as filtering, sorting, and aggregating are commonly used, advanced transformation methods offer more sophisticated capabilities for handling complex data processing tasks. Next, we explore various advanced transformation methods and techniques used in data engineering and analytics.

CLI Command to Explore Advanced Transformation Methods:

bashCopy code

$ explore-advanced-transformation-methods

1. Join Operations

Join operations are fundamental transformation techniques used to combine data from multiple sources based on common keys or attributes. While basic join operations such as inner, outer, left, and right joins are commonly used, advanced join techniques include self-joins, cross-joins, and semi-joins. These techniques enable analysts to merge datasets with different structures, granularity, and formats, allowing for comprehensive data integration and analysis.

CLI Command for Join Operations:

bashCopy code

$ join-operations

2. Window Functions

Window functions, also known as analytic functions or windowing functions, are advanced transformation methods used to perform calculations over a sliding window of rows in a dataset. Window functions enable analysts to calculate

173

cumulative totals, moving averages, rank results, and identify patterns within ordered partitions of data. These functions provide powerful capabilities for performing complex analytical tasks and gaining insights into data distributions and trends.

CLI Command for Window Functions:

bashCopy code

$ window-functions

3. Pivot and Unpivot

Pivoting and unpivoting are transformation techniques used to restructure data from a long format to a wide format (pivoting) or vice versa (unpivoting). Pivoting involves rotating rows into columns based on unique values in a specified column, while unpivoting involves converting columns into rows. These techniques are commonly used in data analysis and reporting to transform data into a format suitable for visualization and interpretation.

CLI Command for Pivot and Unpivot:

bashCopy code

$ pivot-unpivot

4. Recursive Queries

Recursive queries, also known as hierarchical queries or common table expressions (CTEs), are advanced transformation methods used to traverse hierarchical or recursive data structures. Recursive queries enable analysts to perform operations such as hierarchical traversal, pathfinding, and tree aggregations within a dataset. These techniques are commonly used in applications such as organizational hierarchies, bill of materials, and network analysis.

CLI Command for Recursive Queries:

bashCopy code

$ recursive-queries

5. Data Reshaping

Data reshaping techniques involve restructuring datasets to transform data from one shape or structure to another. This may include melting, stacking, or pivoting datasets to convert between wide and long formats or reshape data for specific analysis tasks. Data reshaping techniques are commonly used in data preprocessing and preparation to prepare datasets for analysis and visualization.

CLI Command for Data Reshaping:

bashCopy code

```
$ data-reshaping
```

6. Regular Expressions

Regular expressions, or regex, are powerful transformation tools used to search for and manipulate text patterns within datasets. Regular expressions enable analysts to perform complex string matching, substitution, and extraction operations based on user-defined patterns and rules. These techniques are commonly used in data cleansing, text processing, and pattern recognition tasks.

CLI Command for Regular Expressions:

bashCopy code

```
$ regular-expressions
```

7. Custom Functions and User-Defined Transformations

Custom functions and user-defined transformations allow analysts to define and apply custom logic and operations to datasets. This may involve writing user-defined functions (UDFs) in programming languages such as Python, R, or SQL to perform specialized calculations, transformations, or validations. Custom functions enable analysts to implement domain-specific business rules and algorithms tailored to their specific requirements.

CLI Command for Custom Functions and UDFs:

bashCopy code

$ custom-functions-udfs

8. Data Integration and Wrangling Tools

Data integration and wrangling tools provide graphical interfaces and workflows for performing advanced data transformation tasks. These tools enable analysts to visually design data transformation pipelines, apply transformations, and automate data processing tasks without writing code. Data integration tools often include features such as data profiling, schema mapping, and data lineage to facilitate data preparation and integration processes.

CLI Command for Data Integration and Wrangling Tools:

bashCopy code

$ data-integration-wrangling-tools

9. Parallel Processing and Distributed Computing

Parallel processing and distributed computing techniques enable analysts to perform large-scale data transformations and processing tasks efficiently across distributed computing clusters. These techniques leverage parallelism and distributed computing frameworks such as Apache Spark, Hadoop, or Dask to divide data processing tasks into smaller, parallelizable units and execute them in parallel across multiple nodes or processors. Parallel processing techniques improve performance and scalability for handling big data transformation tasks.

CLI Command for Parallel Processing and Distributed Computing:

bashCopy code

$ parallel-processing-distributed-computing

10. Data Streaming and Real-Time Transformation

Data streaming and real-time transformation techniques enable analysts to process and transform data streams in real-time as they are ingested into the system. This may involve applying streaming analytics, complex event processing (CEP), or real-time processing frameworks such as Apache Kafka, Flink, or Spark Streaming to perform continuous data transformation and analysis. Real-time transformation techniques are essential for applications requiring low-latency processing and immediate insights from streaming data sources.

CLI Command for Data Streaming and Real-Time Transformation:

bashCopy code

$ data-streaming-real-time-transformation

In summary, advanced transformation methods provide powerful capabilities for manipulating and converting data to meet analysis and reporting requirements. By employing techniques such as window functions, recursive queries, regular expressions, and custom transformations, analysts can perform complex data processing tasks and derive valuable insights from diverse datasets. Effective use of advanced transformation methods enables organizations to unlock the full potential of their data assets and drive informed decision-making and innovation.

Handling Complex Data Transformation Scenarios

Data transformation is a critical aspect of the data processing pipeline, enabling organizations to convert raw data into a format suitable for analysis, reporting, and decision-making. However, as datasets grow in size and complexity, the challenges associated with data transformation become more pronounced. Next, we delve into strategies and techniques for handling complex data transformation scenarios, including dealing with unstructured data, managing schema evolution, and addressing data quality issues.

CLI Command to Explore Complex Data Transformation Scenarios:

bashCopy code

$ explore-complex-data-transformation

1. Dealing with Unstructured Data

One of the most common challenges in data transformation is dealing with unstructured or semi-structured data formats such as text, JSON, XML, or binary data. Unstructured data lacks a predefined schema, making it challenging to process and analyze using traditional relational database techniques. To handle unstructured data, organizations often employ techniques such as data parsing, text extraction, and schema inference to extract structured information from unstructured sources.

CLI Command for Dealing with Unstructured Data:

bashCopy code

$ handle-unstructured-data

2. Managing Schema Evolution

Schema evolution refers to the process of managing changes to the structure and definition of datasets over time. As data sources evolve and business requirements change, organizations must adapt their data transformation processes to accommodate schema changes while maintaining compatibility with existing data consumers. Techniques for managing schema evolution include versioning, backward compatibility, schema validation, and data migration strategies to ensure smooth transitions and minimize disruptions to downstream systems.

CLI Command for Managing Schema Evolution:

bashCopy code

$ manage-schema-evolution

3. Addressing Data Quality Issues

Data quality issues such as missing values, outliers, duplicates, and inconsistencies are common challenges in data transformation processes. Poor data quality can lead to inaccurate analysis, unreliable insights, and decision-making errors. To address data quality issues, organizations implement data cleansing, validation, and enrichment techniques to identify and correct errors, standardize data formats, and improve overall data quality.

CLI Command for Addressing Data Quality Issues:
bashCopy code

```
$ address-data-quality-issues
```

4. Handling Complex Transformations

Complex data transformation scenarios often involve multiple steps and dependencies, requiring organizations to implement robust processing pipelines to handle diverse data sources and processing requirements. Techniques for handling complex transformations include workflow orchestration, dependency management, error handling, and retry mechanisms to ensure the reliability and fault tolerance of data transformation pipelines.

CLI Command for Handling Complex Transformations:
bashCopy code

```
$ handle-complex-transformations
```

5. Scalability and Performance Optimization

Scalability and performance optimization are critical considerations in handling complex data transformation scenarios, particularly when dealing with large volumes of data or processing intensive workloads. Organizations employ techniques such as parallel processing, distributed computing, caching, and resource optimization to improve the scalability, throughput, and efficiency of data transformation pipelines.

CLI Command for Scalability and Performance Optimization:

bashCopy code

$ optimize-scalability-performance

6. Error Handling and Fault Tolerance

Error handling and fault tolerance mechanisms are essential for ensuring the reliability and resilience of data transformation processes. Organizations implement techniques such as error detection, logging, monitoring, and automatic recovery mechanisms to handle exceptions, mitigate failures, and maintain data integrity in the face of errors or disruptions.

CLI Command for Error Handling and Fault Tolerance:

bashCopy code

$ handle-errors-fault-tolerance

7. Real-time Data Transformation

Real-time data transformation involves processing and transforming data streams in real-time as they are ingested into the system. Techniques for real-time data transformation include stream processing, complex event processing (CEP), and microbatch processing to enable immediate insights and actions based on streaming data sources.

CLI Command for Real-time Data Transformation:

bashCopy code

$ real-time-data-transformation

8. Compliance and Governance

Compliance and governance considerations are paramount in handling complex data transformation scenarios, particularly in regulated industries or environments with strict data privacy requirements. Organizations implement techniques such as data lineage tracking, audit logging, access control, and encryption to ensure compliance with regulatory standards and protect sensitive data throughout the transformation process.

CLI Command for Compliance and Governance:

bashCopy code

```
$ ensure-compliance-governance
```

In summary, handling complex data transformation scenarios requires organizations to employ a combination of strategies, techniques, and best practices to overcome challenges related to unstructured data, schema evolution, data quality issues, scalability, performance, error handling, and compliance. By implementing robust data transformation processes and leveraging advanced technologies and methodologies, organizations can ensure the reliability, efficiency, and effectiveness of their data transformation initiatives, ultimately enabling them to derive actionable insights and drive business success.

Chapter 5: Loading Data into the Data Warehouse

Loading data into a data warehouse is a critical step in the data processing pipeline, enabling organizations to store, organize, and analyze vast amounts of structured and unstructured data. When designing loading processes, data engineers must consider various strategies to efficiently transfer data from source systems into the data warehouse. Two primary loading strategies commonly employed are full load and incremental load. Next, we explore these strategies, their benefits, challenges, and best practices for implementation.

CLI Command to Explore Loading Strategies:

bashCopy code

```
$ explore-loading-strategies
```

1. Full Load

Full load, also known as bulk load or initial load, involves transferring the entire dataset from source systems to the data warehouse during each loading cycle. In a full load scenario, all existing data in the target tables is replaced or truncated before loading the new dataset. Full load is typically used for initial data population or when the entire dataset needs to be refreshed due to schema changes or data quality issues.

CLI Command for Full Load:

bashCopy code

```
$ full-load
```

Benefits of Full Load:

Simplicity: Full load processes are straightforward to implement and manage since they involve transferring the entire dataset without incremental updates.

Data Consistency: By replacing existing data with fresh data during each load cycle, full load ensures data consistency and eliminates the risk of data inconsistency or corruption.

Challenges of Full Load:

Resource Intensive: Full load processes can be resource-intensive, especially for large datasets, as they require transferring and processing the entire dataset each time.

Increased Downtime: Performing full load operations may result in increased downtime for the data warehouse, impacting system availability and accessibility.

Best Practices for Full Load:

Schedule Off-Peak Hours: Schedule full load processes during off-peak hours to minimize the impact on system performance and user access.

Monitor Performance: Monitor the performance of full load processes regularly to identify bottlenecks and optimize resource utilization.

Implement Data Validation: Implement data validation checks to ensure the integrity and accuracy of the loaded data after each full load operation.

2. Incremental Load

Incremental load, also known as delta load or change data capture (CDC), involves transferring only the changes or updates made to the source data since the last load cycle. In an incremental load scenario, only new or modified records are transferred and merged with the existing data in the target tables, preserving historical data and reducing processing overhead. Incremental load is commonly used for continuous data integration, real-time analytics, and near-real-time reporting.

CLI Command for Incremental Load:

```
bashCopy code
$ incremental-load
```

Benefits of Incremental Load:

Reduced Processing Time: Incremental load processes are more efficient than full load processes since they only transfer and process changes, reducing processing time and resource utilization.

Near-Real-Time Updates: Incremental load enables near-real-time updates to the data warehouse, allowing organizations to analyze the latest data and make timely decisions.

Preserved History: Incremental load preserves historical data in the data warehouse, enabling trend analysis, historical reporting, and auditing.

Challenges of Incremental Load:

Complexity: Implementing incremental load processes may require additional complexity, such as tracking changes, detecting deltas, and managing data synchronization between source and target systems.

Data Consistency: Ensuring data consistency and integrity across incremental load cycles can be challenging, particularly when dealing with concurrent updates or conflicting changes.

Best Practices for Incremental Load:

Use Change Data Capture (CDC): Implement change data capture techniques to identify and capture incremental changes from source systems efficiently.

Maintain Data Quality: Implement data quality checks and validation rules to ensure the accuracy and consistency of incremental data updates.

Monitor Latency: Monitor the latency of incremental load processes to ensure timely data updates and minimize data staleness in the data warehouse.

In summary, choosing the right loading strategy is essential for efficient and reliable data warehousing operations. While full load offers simplicity and data consistency, incremental load provides efficiency, near-real-time updates, and preserved history. By understanding the benefits, challenges, and best practices associated with each loading strategy, organizations can design robust loading processes that meet their data integration, analysis, and reporting requirements effectively. Ultimately, the choice between full load and incremental load depends on factors such as data volume, frequency of updates, latency requirements, and resource constraints, and organizations must carefully evaluate their needs to determine the most suitable approach.

Techniques for Efficient Data Loading

Efficient data loading is crucial for maintaining the performance and scalability of a data warehouse. As data volumes continue to grow exponentially, organizations need to employ techniques that streamline the process of loading data into their data warehouses. Next, we explore various techniques and best practices for efficient data loading, including parallel loading, data partitioning, compression, and pre-aggregation.

CLI Command to Explore Efficient Data Loading Techniques:

bashCopy code

$ explore-efficient-data-loading-techniques

1. Parallel Loading

Parallel loading involves dividing the data loading process into multiple concurrent tasks that run simultaneously, leveraging the processing power of multiple resources to speed up the overall loading time. By parallelizing the loading process, organizations can take advantage of multi-core processors, distributed computing environments, and parallel database architectures to achieve significant performance improvements.

CLI Command for Parallel Loading:

bashCopy code

$ parallel-load

Benefits of Parallel Loading:

Reduced Loading Time: Parallel loading distributes the workload across multiple threads or nodes, reducing the overall loading time compared to sequential loading.

Scalability: Parallel loading scales seamlessly with increasing data volumes, allowing organizations to load large datasets efficiently without compromising performance.

Resource Utilization: Parallel loading maximizes resource utilization by leveraging the available processing power of multiple cores or nodes, optimizing hardware resources.

Challenges of Parallel Loading:

Data Dependency: Parallel loading requires careful management of data dependencies and synchronization to ensure data consistency and integrity across parallel tasks.

Overhead: Implementing parallel loading may introduce additional overhead, such as coordination overhead, network overhead, and contention for shared resources.

Best Practices for Parallel Loading:

Partition Data: Partition the dataset into smaller chunks based on a partition key or criteria to enable parallel processing while minimizing data dependencies.

Load Balancing: Implement load balancing strategies to evenly distribute the workload across parallel tasks and prevent resource bottlenecks.

Monitoring and Optimization: Monitor the performance of parallel loading processes and optimize parallelism settings based on workload characteristics and system resources.

2. Data Partitioning

Data partitioning involves dividing a large dataset into smaller partitions or segments based on predefined criteria, such as range partitioning, hash partitioning, or list partitioning. Partitioning enables parallel processing, efficient data retrieval, and improved query performance by limiting the amount of data scanned or processed for each operation.

CLI Command for Data Partitioning:

bashCopy code

$ data-partitioning

Benefits of Data Partitioning:

Enhanced Performance: Data partitioning improves query performance by reducing the amount of data scanned or processed for each query, resulting in faster response times.

Scalability: Partitioning enables horizontal scalability by distributing data across multiple partitions, allowing organizations to scale their data warehouses seamlessly as data volumes grow.

Data Isolation: Partitioning provides logical data isolation, enabling organizations to manage and access data more efficiently based on partition criteria.

Challenges of Data Partitioning:

Partitioning Key Selection: Choosing the right partition key is crucial for effective data partitioning, as it impacts query performance, data distribution, and maintenance overhead.

Data Skew: Imbalanced data distribution across partitions, known as data skew, can lead to uneven query execution times and resource contention issues.

Best Practices for Data Partitioning:

Understand Query Patterns: Analyze query patterns and access patterns to identify suitable partitioning keys that align with query filtering conditions and data distribution characteristics.

Monitor Partition Sizes: Monitor partition sizes regularly and rebalance partitions as needed to prevent data skew and optimize query performance.

Use Composite Partitioning: Consider using composite partitioning strategies that combine multiple partitioning methods, such as range-hash partitioning or range-list partitioning, to achieve finer data segmentation and flexibility.

3. Compression

Compression techniques reduce the storage footprint of data by encoding it in a more space-efficient format, enabling organizations to store and transfer data more efficiently. Compression can be applied to both data files and indexes, reducing storage costs, improving I/O performance, and speeding up data loading and retrieval operations.

CLI Command for Compression:

bashCopy code

$ compression-techniques

Benefits of Compression:

Reduced Storage Costs: Compression reduces the storage footprint of data, resulting in lower storage costs and improved resource utilization.

Improved Performance: Compressed data requires less disk space and I/O bandwidth, leading to faster data loading, retrieval, and query execution times.

Efficient Data Transfer: Compressed data consumes less network bandwidth during data transfer operations, making it ideal for distributed environments and data replication scenarios.

Challenges of Compression:

Compression Overhead: Compression introduces additional CPU overhead during data encoding and decoding operations, which can impact system performance, especially on resource-constrained systems.

Compression Ratios: Achieving optimal compression ratios depends on factors such as data characteristics, compression algorithms, and compression settings, making it challenging to predict compression gains accurately.

Best Practices for Compression:

Choose Appropriate Compression Algorithms: Select compression algorithms based on data characteristics, such as text data, numeric data, or binary data, to achieve optimal compression ratios and performance.

Monitor Compression Performance: Monitor the performance impact of compression techniques on data loading, query execution, and system resources to identify potential bottlenecks and optimize compression settings.

Balance Compression and CPU Resources: Strike a balance between compression gains and CPU overhead by experimenting with different compression levels and algorithms to find the optimal configuration for your workload.

4. Pre-aggregation

Pre-aggregation involves aggregating and summarizing data at various levels of granularity before loading it into the data warehouse, reducing the amount of raw data stored and improving query performance for common aggregation queries. Pre-aggregation techniques include roll-up, drill-down, and cube-based aggregations, which enable organizations to generate precomputed summaries of data for faster analytical queries.

CLI Command for Pre-aggregation:

bashCopy code

$ pre-aggregation

Benefits of Pre-aggregation:

Improved Query Performance: Pre-aggregated data enables faster query performance by providing precomputed summaries of data at different levels of granularity, reducing the need for expensive aggregation operations at query time.

Reduced Storage Requirements: Pre-aggregation reduces the storage footprint of data by storing aggregated summaries instead of raw, detailed data, resulting in lower storage costs and improved resource utilization.

Enhanced Scalability: Pre-aggregation improves the scalability of data warehouses by offloading computation-intensive aggregation tasks to the ETL process, freeing up resources for concurrent query processing and analysis.

Challenges of Pre-aggregation:

Data Freshness: Pre-aggregated data may become stale over time, especially for rapidly changing or volatile datasets, requiring organizations to balance query performance with data freshness requirements.

Data Granularity: Determining the appropriate level of aggregation and granularity for pre-aggregated data requires careful consideration of business requirements, query patterns, and performance trade-offs.

Best Practices for Pre-aggregation:

Understand Query Workloads: Analyze query workloads and access patterns to identify common aggregation queries and determine the appropriate levels of pre-aggregation needed to optimize query performance.

Incremental Aggregation: Implement incremental aggregation techniques to update pre-aggregated summaries incrementally as new data arrives, minimizing the impact on data freshness and reducing computational overhead.

Monitor Query Performance: Monitor the performance of pre-aggregated queries regularly to identify opportunities for optimization and adjust aggregation levels as needed to meet performance targets.

In summary, efficient data loading is essential for maintaining the performance, scalability, and cost-effectiveness of data warehouse operations. By employing techniques such as parallel loading, data partitioning, compression, and pre-aggregation, organizations can optimize the process of loading data into their data warehouses, improve query performance, reduce storage costs, and enhance overall system efficiency. However, selecting the right combination of techniques requires careful consideration of factors such as data characteristics, query patterns, performance requirements, and resource constraints. By understanding the benefits, challenges, and best practices associated with each technique, organizations can design robust data loading processes that meet their specific business needs and drive actionable insights from their data assets.

Chapter 6: Incremental Loading and Change Data Capture (CDC)

Incremental loading is a crucial technique in data warehousing that involves updating the data warehouse with only the changes or new data since the last update, rather than reloading the entire dataset. This approach reduces the time and resources required for data loading, improves data freshness, and enables near-real-time analytics. Next, we explore the concept of incremental loading, its benefits, challenges, best practices, and implementation strategies.

CLI Command to Explore Incremental Loading:

bashCopy code

$ explore-incremental-loading

1. The Need for Incremental Loading

In traditional data warehousing scenarios, where large volumes of data are involved, reloading the entire dataset during each update can be inefficient and time-consuming. Incremental loading addresses this challenge by selectively loading only the data that has changed or is new since the last update. This approach ensures that the data warehouse reflects the most up-to-date information while minimizing the processing overhead.

CLI Command for Understanding the Need for Incremental Loading:

bashCopy code

$ understand-incremental-loading-need

2. Benefits of Incremental Loading

Incremental loading offers several benefits to organizations, including:

Reduced Processing Time: By loading only the incremental changes, organizations can significantly reduce the time required for data loading, resulting in faster data availability for analytics and reporting.

Improved Data Freshness: Incremental loading ensures that the data warehouse contains the latest information, enabling near-real-time analytics and decision-making.

Optimal Resource Utilization: Selective data loading reduces the computational and storage resources needed for data warehousing operations, leading to improved system efficiency and cost-effectiveness.

CLI Command for Exploring the Benefits of Incremental Loading:

bashCopy code

$ explore-incremental-loading-benefits

3. Challenges of Incremental Loading

While incremental loading offers numerous benefits, it also presents certain challenges, including:

Data Integrity: Ensuring data integrity and consistency during incremental updates can be challenging, especially when dealing with complex data relationships and dependencies.

Change Tracking: Tracking changes in source data and identifying incremental updates accurately require robust change detection mechanisms and metadata management capabilities.

Performance Overhead: Implementing incremental loading may introduce additional performance overhead, such as query complexity, resource contention, and synchronization issues.

CLI Command for Understanding the Challenges of Incremental Loading:

bashCopy code

$ understand-incremental-loading-challenges

4. Best Practices for Incremental Loading

To overcome the challenges associated with incremental loading and maximize its benefits, organizations should follow best practices such as:

Implementing Change Data Capture (CDC): Utilize CDC techniques to capture and track changes in source data, enabling selective loading of incremental updates.

Using Timestamps or Versioning: Incorporate timestamp-based or versioning mechanisms to identify and timestamp changes in source data, facilitating incremental loading.

Ensuring Data Consistency: Implement validation checks and data integrity constraints to ensure the consistency and correctness of incrementally loaded data.

Monitoring and Optimization: Regularly monitor incremental loading processes, performance metrics, and data quality to identify bottlenecks, optimize workflows, and ensure efficient operation.

CLI Command for Implementing Best Practices for Incremental Loading:

bashCopy code

$ implement-incremental-loading-best-practices

5. Implementation Strategies for Incremental Loading

Organizations can implement incremental loading using various strategies, including:

Key-Based Incremental Loading: Use primary keys or unique identifiers to identify and load only the records that have changed or are new since the last update.

Date-Based Incremental Loading: Employ date or timestamp columns to identify and load records that have been modified or added within a specific time window.

CDC-Based Incremental Loading: Leverage CDC mechanisms provided by database systems or ETL tools to capture and replicate changes from source systems to the data warehouse.

CLI Command for Implementing Incremental Loading Strategies:

bashCopy code

$ implement-incremental-loading-strategies

Incremental loading is a fundamental technique in data warehousing that enables organizations to efficiently update their data warehouses with only the changes or new data since the last update. By adopting incremental loading, organizations can improve data freshness, reduce processing time, optimize resource utilization, and support near-real-time analytics and decision-making. However, implementing incremental loading requires careful consideration of factors such as data integrity, change tracking mechanisms, performance optimization, and implementation strategies. By following best practices and leveraging suitable implementation strategies, organizations can harness the full potential of incremental loading to maintain a robust and up-to-date data warehouse environment.

Change Data Capture (CDC) is a crucial mechanism in data warehousing that enables organizations to capture and track changes made to source data. By identifying and capturing these changes, CDC facilitates the selective extraction and replication of only the modified or new data, allowing for efficient data synchronization between source systems and the data warehouse. Next, we delve into the concept of CDC, its importance, implementation techniques, best practices, and real-world applications.

1. Understanding Change Data Capture

Change Data Capture (CDC) is a process that captures and records data modifications made to source tables in near real-time. It identifies inserts, updates, and deletes performed on source data and records these changes in a persistent log or journal. CDC enables organizations to track the evolution of data over time, maintain data lineage, and replicate changes to downstream systems, including data warehouses, data lakes, and analytical platforms.

CLI Command for Understanding Change Data Capture:
bashCopy code

```
$ understand-change-data-capture
```

2. Importance of Change Data Capture

CDC plays a pivotal role in data warehousing and analytics by offering several benefits, including:

Real-Time Data Integration: By capturing changes as they occur, CDC enables real-time or near-real-time data integration, ensuring that the data warehouse reflects the most up-to-date information.

Efficient Data Synchronization: CDC reduces the overhead of extracting and processing large volumes of data by selectively capturing and replicating only the modified or new data, leading to faster synchronization between source systems and the data warehouse.

Accurate Data Analysis: With CDC, organizations can analyze data changes over time, track historical trends, and gain insights into evolving business processes, customer behavior, and market dynamics.

CLI Command for Exploring the Importance of Change Data Capture:

bashCopy code

$ explore-cdc-importance

3. Implementation Techniques for Change Data Capture

There are several techniques for implementing Change Data Capture, including:

Database Triggers: Utilize database triggers to capture data changes at the row level by automatically executing predefined actions (e.g., logging changes to a separate table) when specific data manipulation operations occur.

Log-Based CDC: Leverage transaction logs or redo logs provided by database management systems to capture data changes at the database level, enabling comprehensive and low-latency change capture without impacting source system performance.

Timestamp-Based CDC: Use timestamp columns or system-generated timestamps to track changes in source data, allowing for incremental extraction and replication of data based on the last modified timestamp.

CLI Command for Implementing Change Data Capture Techniques:

bashCopy code

$ implement-cdc-techniques

4. Best Practices for Change Data Capture

To maximize the effectiveness of Change Data Capture, organizations should follow best practices such as:

Data Validation: Implement robust validation checks to ensure data integrity and consistency during the CDC process, including error handling, data reconciliation, and conflict resolution mechanisms.

Incremental Loading: Integrate CDC with incremental loading techniques to selectively extract and replicate only the changed or new data, minimizing processing overhead and ensuring efficient data synchronization.

Monitoring and Auditing: Establish monitoring and auditing mechanisms to track CDC performance, detect anomalies or failures, and maintain visibility into data lineage, change history, and replication status.

CLI Command for Implementing Best Practices for Change Data Capture:

bashCopy code

```
$ implement-cdc-best-practices
```

5. Real-World Applications of Change Data Capture

CDC finds applications across various industries and use cases, including:

Financial Services: Banks and financial institutions use CDC to track changes in transaction data, detect fraudulent activities, and ensure regulatory compliance.

Retail and E-commerce: Retailers leverage CDC to monitor inventory levels, track sales transactions, and analyze customer purchase behavior in real-time.

Healthcare: Healthcare organizations use CDC to capture and analyze patient data, monitor treatment outcomes, and support clinical decision-making processes.

CLI Command for Exploring Real-World Applications of Change Data Capture:

bashCopy code

```
$ explore-cdc-applications
```

Change Data Capture (CDC) is a fundamental technique in data warehousing that enables organizations to capture and track changes made to source data in near real-time. By implementing CDC, organizations can achieve real-time data integration, efficient data synchronization, and accurate data analysis, driving informed decision-making and business agility. However, successful implementation of CDC requires careful consideration of implementation techniques, best practices, and real-world applications. By adopting CDC and adhering to best practices, organizations can maintain a synchronized and up-to-date data environment that supports their analytical and operational needs.

Chapter 7: Managing ETL Performance and Scalability

Performance optimization is a critical aspect of data warehousing that aims to enhance the speed, efficiency, and scalability of data processing operations. Next, we explore various strategies and techniques for optimizing the performance of data warehousing systems, including query optimization, indexing, partitioning, compression, and parallel processing.

1. Query Optimization

Query optimization involves improving the performance of SQL queries executed against the data warehouse by minimizing resource consumption and maximizing query execution speed. Techniques for query optimization include:

Query Rewriting: Rewriting complex queries to simpler forms that yield the same results but require fewer computational resources.

Query Plan Analysis: Analyzing query execution plans generated by the database optimizer to identify potential bottlenecks and optimize query execution paths.

Indexing: Creating appropriate indexes on columns frequently used in query predicates to facilitate faster data retrieval.

CLI Command for Query Optimization:

bashCopy code

```
$ optimize-queries
```

2. Indexing

Indexing is a technique used to improve the speed of data retrieval operations by creating data structures that enable quick access to specific rows based on indexed columns. Types of indexes commonly used in data warehousing include:

B-tree Indexes: Suitable for range queries and equality predicates, B-tree indexes provide efficient access to data based on sorted key values.

Bitmap Indexes: Ideal for low cardinality columns, bitmap indexes use bitmaps to represent the presence or absence of rows matching each distinct column value.

Hash Indexes: Hash indexes use hash functions to map column values to index keys, providing fast access to data with constant-time lookups.

CLI Command for Indexing:

bashCopy code

```
$ create-indexes
```

3. Partitioning

Partitioning involves dividing large tables or indexes into smaller, more manageable segments called partitions based on predefined criteria such as range, list, or hash. Partitioning offers several benefits for performance optimization, including:

Reduced I/O Operations: Partitioning allows data to be accessed and manipulated at a finer granularity, resulting in reduced I/O overhead and improved query performance.

Enhanced Parallelism: Partitioned tables or indexes can be processed in parallel by multiple threads or processes, enabling faster data retrieval and processing.

Improved Data Management: Partitioning facilitates efficient data management, backup, and maintenance operations by isolating and managing data subsets independently.

CLI Command for Partitioning:

```
bashCopy code
$ partition-tables
```

4. Compression

Compression techniques are used to reduce the storage footprint of data in the data warehouse, thereby improving storage efficiency and reducing I/O latency. Common compression techniques include:

Columnar Compression: Storing column values in a compressed format optimized for analytical queries, such as dictionary encoding, run-length encoding, and delta encoding.

Block-Level Compression: Compressing data blocks or pages at the storage level using algorithms like gzip, Snappy, or LZ4 to reduce disk space utilization and improve I/O performance.

Hybrid Compression: Combining multiple compression algorithms or strategies to achieve a balance between compression ratio, decompression overhead, and query performance.

CLI Command for Compression:

```
bashCopy code
$ compress-data
```

5. Parallel Processing

Parallel processing involves distributing data processing tasks across multiple CPU cores, nodes, or clusters to achieve faster query execution and improved system scalability. Techniques for parallel processing include:

Parallel Query Execution: Executing queries in parallel across multiple threads or processes to leverage the computational resources of modern multi-core CPUs.

Distributed Processing: Distributing query execution tasks across multiple nodes or servers in a distributed computing environment, such as Apache Hadoop or Apache Spark clusters.

Data Parallelism: Breaking down data processing tasks into smaller chunks and processing them in parallel across distributed computing resources to achieve scalable and efficient data processing.

CLI Command for Parallel Processing:

bashCopy code

```
$ parallelize-processing
```

Performance optimization is essential for ensuring the efficiency, scalability, and responsiveness of data warehousing systems. By employing strategies such as query optimization, indexing, partitioning, compression, and parallel processing, organizations can enhance the speed, efficiency, and scalability of their data processing operations, leading to improved query performance, reduced resource consumption, and enhanced user experience. However, selecting the appropriate optimization techniques requires careful consideration of factors such as data characteristics, workload patterns, system architecture, and performance objectives. By adopting a holistic approach to performance optimization and leveraging a combination of techniques tailored to their specific requirements, organizations can build robust and high-performance data warehousing environments that meet their analytical and operational needs.

Scalability Considerations in ETL Processes

Scalability is a critical aspect of ETL (Extract, Transform, Load) processes, ensuring that data pipelines can efficiently handle increasing volumes of data while maintaining performance and reliability. Next, we explore various scalability considerations in ETL processes, including data volume, processing speed, resource allocation, and system architecture.

1. Understanding Scalability in ETL Processes

Scalability refers to the ability of an ETL system to accommodate growing data volumes, user loads, and processing requirements without compromising performance or reliability. Scalable ETL processes can effectively handle large datasets, accommodate fluctuating workloads, and scale up or down based on demand.

CLI Command for Understanding Scalability in ETL Processes:

bashCopy code

$ understand-etl-scalability

2. Horizontal Scaling vs. Vertical Scaling

Two primary approaches to scalability are horizontal scaling and vertical scaling:

Horizontal Scaling: Also known as scale-out, horizontal scaling involves adding more nodes or instances to distribute the workload across multiple machines. Horizontal scaling is well-suited for ETL processes with high data volumes and parallelizable tasks.

Vertical Scaling: Also known as scale-up, vertical scaling involves increasing the capacity of individual nodes by upgrading hardware resources such as CPU, memory, or storage. Vertical scaling is suitable for ETL processes with single-threaded or resource-intensive tasks.

CLI Command for Scaling ETL Processes:

bashCopy code

$ scale-etl-horizontal $ scale-etl-vertical

3. Partitioning and Parallelism

Partitioning and parallelism are essential techniques for achieving scalability in ETL processes:

Data Partitioning: Divide large datasets into smaller partitions based on predefined criteria (e.g., range, hash, or list) to distribute processing tasks across multiple nodes or threads.

Parallel Processing: Execute data transformation and loading tasks in parallel across multiple nodes, threads, or cores to leverage the computational resources and achieve faster processing.

CLI Command for Implementing Partitioning and Parallelism:

bashCopy code

$ partition-data $ parallelize-processing

4. Resource Management and Allocation

Effective resource management is crucial for ensuring scalability in ETL processes:

Resource Allocation: Allocate computational resources such as CPU, memory, and storage based on the requirements of individual ETL tasks, workload priorities, and performance objectives.

Dynamic Resource Provisioning: Implement dynamic resource allocation mechanisms that automatically adjust resource allocations based on workload demands, system utilization, and performance metrics.

CLI Command for Resource Management in ETL Processes:

bashCopy code

$ allocate-resources $ provision-dynamic-resources

5. Distributed Computing and Cluster Architecture

Distributed computing and cluster architecture play a vital role in achieving scalability:

Distributed Computing: Distribute ETL tasks across multiple nodes or servers in a distributed computing environment to achieve parallel execution, fault tolerance, and scalability.

Cluster Architecture: Deploy ETL processes on scalable cluster architectures such as Apache Hadoop, Apache Spark, or Kubernetes clusters to leverage distributed computing resources and achieve linear scalability.

CLI Command for Deploying Distributed Computing and Cluster Architecture:

bashCopy code

```
$    deploy-distributed-computing    $    deploy-cluster-architecture
```

Scalability is essential for ensuring that ETL processes can handle increasing data volumes and processing demands while maintaining performance and reliability. By adopting techniques such as horizontal scaling, vertical scaling, partitioning, parallelism, resource management, and distributed computing, organizations can build scalable and robust ETL systems capable of handling large datasets and fluctuating workloads. However, achieving scalability requires careful planning, design, and implementation, considering factors such as data volume, workload patterns, system architecture, and performance objectives. By addressing scalability considerations early in the design phase and continuously monitoring and optimizing ETL processes, organizations can build scalable and future-proof data integration pipelines that meet their evolving business needs.

Chapter 8: ETL Automation and Orchestration

Automation plays a crucial role in streamlining Extract, Transform, Load (ETL) processes, reducing manual intervention, and improving efficiency and reliability. Next, we delve into various tools and techniques for automating ETL processes, including scheduling, workflow orchestration, monitoring, and error handling.

1. Introduction to ETL Automation

ETL automation involves the use of tools and technologies to automate repetitive tasks involved in data extraction, transformation, and loading. Automation streamlines the ETL workflow, reduces human errors, and enables timely and efficient data processing.

CLI Command for ETL Automation:

bashCopy code

```
$ automate-etl
```

2. Scheduling

Scheduling is a fundamental aspect of ETL automation, enabling the execution of ETL jobs at predefined intervals or based on specific events. Common scheduling techniques include:

Time-Based Scheduling: Triggering ETL jobs at scheduled time intervals (e.g., hourly, daily, weekly) using cron jobs or built-in scheduling features of ETL tools.

Event-Based Scheduling: Triggering ETL jobs based on specific events or conditions, such as file arrival, database changes, or API calls, using event-driven architectures or workflow orchestration tools.

CLI Command for Scheduling ETL Jobs:

bashCopy code

```bash
$ schedule-etl-jobs
```

3. Workflow Orchestration

Workflow orchestration involves defining, managing, and executing complex ETL workflows comprising multiple tasks and dependencies. Workflow orchestration tools provide graphical interfaces or DSLs (Domain-Specific Languages) for designing and executing ETL workflows.

CLI Command for Workflow Orchestration:

bashCopy code

```bash
$ orchestrate-workflows
```

4. Monitoring and Alerting

Monitoring and alerting are essential for ensuring the health, performance, and reliability of automated ETL processes. Monitoring tools track key performance metrics, detect anomalies, and trigger alerts or notifications for timely intervention.

CLI Command for Monitoring ETL Processes:

bashCopy code

```bash
$ monitor-etl-processes
```

5. Error Handling and Recovery

Error handling and recovery mechanisms are critical for handling exceptions, errors, and failures encountered during ETL processing. Techniques for error handling include logging, retry mechanisms, error queues, and automated recovery procedures.

CLI Command for Error Handling in ETL Processes:

bashCopy code

```bash
$ handle-errors-etl
```

6. Data Quality Checks

Automated data quality checks ensure that data ingested into the data warehouse meets predefined quality standards and validation rules. Data quality tools perform checks for completeness, accuracy, consistency, and conformity to ensure data integrity.

CLI Command for Data Quality Checks:

bashCopy code

$ perform-data-quality-checks

7. Deployment of ETL Automation Tools

Deploying ETL automation tools involves installing, configuring, and integrating ETL software components into the existing IT infrastructure. Deployment techniques vary based on the selected ETL tools and technologies.

CLI Command for Deploying ETL Automation Tools:

bashCopy code

$ deploy-etl-tools

8. Integration with DevOps Practices

Integrating ETL automation with DevOps practices facilitates continuous integration, deployment, and monitoring of ETL pipelines. DevOps tools and methodologies enable seamless collaboration between development, operations, and data teams.

CLI Command for Integrating ETL with DevOps Practices:

bashCopy code

$ integrate-etl-devops

Automating ETL processes is essential for improving efficiency, reliability, and scalability in data integration workflows. By leveraging tools and techniques for scheduling, workflow orchestration, monitoring, error handling, and data quality checks, organizations can streamline ETL operations, reduce manual effort, and accelerate time-to-insight. However, successful ETL automation requires careful planning, implementation, and continuous monitoring to ensure smooth execution and timely delivery of high-quality data for analytics and decision-making. By adopting a systematic approach to ETL automation and embracing emerging technologies and best practices, organizations can build robust and future-proof data integration pipelines that support their evolving business needs.

Orchestration of ETL Workflows

In the realm of data engineering, orchestrating ETL (Extract, Transform, Load) workflows is a pivotal task that ensures the seamless execution of various data processing tasks. This chapter explores the significance of orchestrating ETL workflows, techniques for workflow management, and the role of orchestration tools in streamlining data pipelines.

1. Introduction to ETL Workflow Orchestration

ETL workflow orchestration involves coordinating and managing the execution of multiple tasks within a data pipeline. It encompasses defining dependencies between tasks, scheduling their execution, monitoring progress, and handling errors or failures.

CLI Command for Orchestration Introduction:

bashCopy code

$ orchestration-intro

2. Workflow Specification

Effective orchestration begins with clear specification of ETL workflows. This includes defining the sequence of tasks, their dependencies, input/output data sources, and expected outcomes. Workflow specification serves as a blueprint for orchestrating data pipelines.

CLI Command for Workflow Specification:

```
bashCopy code
$ specify-workflow
```

3. Task Dependency Management

Task dependency management ensures that tasks are executed in the correct order based on their dependencies. Tasks may have upstream dependencies (tasks that must be completed before they start) and downstream dependencies (tasks that rely on their completion).

CLI Command for Task Dependency Management:

```
bashCopy code
$ manage-task-dependencies
```

4. Scheduling and Execution

Scheduling involves determining when each task within the workflow should be executed. Schedulers allow tasks to be triggered based on time intervals, event triggers, or the completion of other tasks. Efficient scheduling ensures timely execution of ETL processes.

CLI Command for Scheduling and Execution:

```
bashCopy code
$ schedule-etl-tasks
```

5. Parallelism and Concurrency

Parallelism and concurrency enhance the efficiency of ETL workflows by executing multiple tasks simultaneously. Parallel execution reduces overall processing time and enables better utilization of computing resources.

CLI Command for Parallelism and Concurrency:

```
bashCopy code
$ execute-tasks-parallel
```

6. Error Handling and Recovery

Robust error handling mechanisms are essential for managing failures and exceptions during ETL workflow execution. Techniques such as retrying failed tasks, logging errors, and triggering alerts ensure data integrity and reliability.

CLI Command for Error Handling and Recovery:

bashCopy code

```
$ handle-errors-recovery
```

7. Monitoring and Reporting

Monitoring tools provide visibility into the progress and performance of ETL workflows. Real-time monitoring, logging, and reporting capabilities enable data engineers to track job statuses, identify bottlenecks, and troubleshoot issues promptly.

CLI Command for Monitoring and Reporting:

bashCopy code

```
$ monitor-etl-workflows
```

8. Workflow Automation Tools

Several tools and frameworks are available for orchestrating ETL workflows, each offering unique features and capabilities. Popular workflow automation tools include Apache Airflow, Apache NiFi, Luigi, and AWS Step Functions.

CLI Command for Workflow Automation Tools:

bashCopy code

```
$ explore-orchestration-tools
```

9. Deployment Considerations

Deploying an orchestration solution involves configuring the infrastructure, setting up the workflow definitions, and integrating with other data processing components. Deployment considerations include scalability, fault tolerance, and integration with existing systems.

CLI Command for Deployment Considerations:

bashCopy code

$ deploy-orchestration-solution

10. Best Practices

Adhering to best practices is essential for designing and managing ETL workflows effectively. Best practices include modularizing workflows, documenting processes, version control, testing, and continuous optimization.

CLI Command for Best Practices:

bashCopy code

$ follow-orchestration-best-practices

Orchestrating ETL workflows is a critical aspect of data engineering, ensuring the efficient and reliable execution of data processing tasks. By effectively managing task dependencies, scheduling execution, handling errors, and monitoring performance, organizations can streamline their data pipelines and derive valuable insights from their data. By embracing workflow orchestration tools and following best practices, data engineers can build robust and scalable ETL solutions that meet the evolving needs of their organizations.

Chapter 9: Error Handling and Data Quality Assurance in ETL

Error handling is a critical aspect of data engineering, ensuring the reliability and integrity of data processing pipelines. Next, we explore various error handling strategies, techniques, and best practices employed in data engineering workflows.

1. Introduction to Error Handling

Error handling is the process of identifying, managing, and resolving errors or exceptions that occur during data processing. Errors can arise due to various reasons, including data quality issues, infrastructure failures, or software bugs. Effective error handling is essential for maintaining data integrity and ensuring the robustness of data pipelines.

CLI Command for Introduction to Error Handling:

bashCopy code

```
$ error-handling-intro
```

2. Logging and Monitoring

Logging and monitoring play a crucial role in error handling, providing visibility into the execution of data pipelines and capturing information about errors when they occur. Logging frameworks such as Log4j, Logback, or Python's logging module allow developers to record diagnostic information for troubleshooting purposes.

CLI Command for Logging and Monitoring:

bashCopy code

```
$ enable-logging-monitoring
```

3. Retry Mechanisms

Retry mechanisms are used to automatically retry failed operations, such as database queries or API calls, with the aim of recovering from transient errors. Exponential backoff algorithms, which progressively increase the time between retry attempts, are commonly used to prevent overwhelming the system during periods of high load.

CLI Command for Implementing Retry Mechanisms:

bashCopy code

$ implement-retry-mechanism

4. Dead Letter Queues

Dead letter queues (DLQs) are used to store messages that cannot be processed successfully after a certain number of retries. Messages in the DLQ can be reviewed manually or processed separately to identify and address the underlying issues causing the failures.

CLI Command for Setting Up Dead Letter Queues:

bashCopy code

$ configure-dlq

5. Circuit Breakers

Circuit breakers are a fault-tolerant mechanism used to prevent cascading failures in distributed systems. When a service encounters repeated failures, the circuit breaker trips and temporarily stops sending requests to that service. This helps to prevent overloading the system and allows time for recovery.

CLI Command for Implementing Circuit Breakers:

bashCopy code

$ implement-circuit-breaker

6. Graceful Degradation

Graceful degradation is a strategy that allows a system to continue functioning, albeit with reduced functionality, in the event of failure. For example, a web application might display cached data or a simplified interface if the database is unavailable, rather than crashing completely.

CLI Command for Implementing Graceful Degradation:

bashCopy code

$ enable-graceful-degradation

7. Alerting and Notification

Alerting and notification mechanisms are essential for timely detection and response to errors in data processing pipelines. Monitoring systems can be configured to trigger alerts via email, SMS, or integration with collaboration tools like Slack or Microsoft Teams when predefined thresholds or conditions are met.

CLI Command for Setting Up Alerting and Notification:

bashCopy code

$ configure-alerting-notification

8. Automated Testing

Automated testing is a proactive approach to error handling, helping to identify and prevent errors before they occur in production. Unit tests, integration tests, and end-to-end tests verify the correctness of data transformations, data validations, and system interactions, reducing the likelihood of errors slipping through undetected.

CLI Command for Implementing Automated Testing:

bashCopy code

$ automate-testing

9. Documentation and Knowledge Sharing

Comprehensive documentation and knowledge sharing practices help to facilitate effective error handling across teams. Documentation should include information about common errors, troubleshooting procedures, and best practices for handling different types of failures.

CLI Command for Documenting Error Handling Procedures:

bashCopy code

$ document-error-handling

10. Continuous Improvement

Error handling strategies should be continuously evaluated and refined based on feedback, monitoring data, and lessons learned from past incidents. Regular retrospectives and post-mortems help to identify areas for improvement and drive iterative enhancements to error handling processes.

CLI Command for Continuous Improvement of Error Handling:

bashCopy code

$ improve-error-handling

Effective error handling is essential for maintaining the reliability and resilience of data processing pipelines in data engineering. By implementing robust error handling strategies, organizations can minimize the impact of failures, ensure data integrity, and maintain the trustworthiness of their data. By combining proactive measures such as logging, monitoring, and automated testing with reactive mechanisms like retrying, dead letter queues, and circuit breakers, data engineers can build resilient systems capable of handling errors gracefully and recovering quickly from failures.

Ensuring Data Quality Throughout the ETL Process

Maintaining data quality is paramount in any data-driven organization to ensure accurate decision-making and reliable insights. Next, we delve into the significance of data quality throughout the ETL (Extract, Transform, Load) process, exploring techniques, best practices, and tools to ensure data integrity at each stage.

1. Introduction to Data Quality in ETL

Data quality encompasses various dimensions, including accuracy, completeness, consistency, timeliness, and reliability. Ensuring data quality throughout the ETL process is essential to prevent inaccuracies, inconsistencies, and errors from propagating downstream and affecting business decisions.

CLI Command for Introduction to Data Quality in ETL:

bashCopy code

```
$ data-quality-intro
```

2. Data Profiling and Analysis

Data profiling involves analyzing the structure, content, and quality of data sources to identify anomalies, inconsistencies, and potential issues. Profiling tools can automatically scan datasets to uncover missing values, duplicates, outliers, and other data anomalies.

CLI Command for Data Profiling and Analysis:

bashCopy code

```
$ profile-data
```

3. Data Cleansing and Standardization

Data cleansing techniques are employed to rectify errors, inconsistencies, and inaccuracies in the data. This may include removing duplicates, correcting misspellings, standardizing formats, and validating data against predefined rules or constraints.

CLI Command for Data Cleansing and Standardization:

bashCopy code

```
$ cleanse-data
```

4. Data Validation and Quality Checks

Data validation ensures that data meets predefined quality criteria and business rules. This involves performing validation checks such as range validation, format validation, referential integrity checks, and cross-field validations to identify and flag erroneous or suspicious data.

CLI Command for Data Validation and Quality Checks:

bashCopy code

```
$ validate-data
```

5. Error Handling and Reconciliation

Effective error handling mechanisms are crucial for identifying, logging, and resolving data quality issues encountered during the ETL process. Error logs should capture details about the nature of errors, affected records, and actions taken to rectify them. Reconciliation processes compare data between source and target systems to ensure consistency and accuracy.

CLI Command for Error Handling and Reconciliation:

bashCopy code

```
$ handle-errors-reconciliation
```

6. Data Governance and Compliance

Data governance frameworks establish policies, processes, and controls to ensure the quality, security, and integrity of data assets. Compliance with regulatory requirements such as GDPR, HIPAA, or SOX mandates adherence to data governance principles, including data privacy, security, and auditability.

CLI Command for Data Governance and Compliance:

bashCopy code

```
$ enforce-data-governance
```

7. Metadata Management

Metadata management involves capturing, cataloging, and managing metadata—descriptive information about data assets. Metadata repositories provide insights into data lineage, data quality metrics, transformation logic, and data usage, facilitating better understanding and governance of data assets.

CLI Command for Metadata Management:
bashCopy code

$ manage-metadata

8. Data Quality Metrics and Monitoring

Defining and tracking data quality metrics enables organizations to assess and monitor the overall health of their data. Metrics such as completeness, accuracy, consistency, and timeliness provide quantitative measures of data quality and help identify areas for improvement.

CLI Command for Data Quality Metrics and Monitoring:
bashCopy code

$ monitor-data-quality

9. Continuous Improvement and Feedback Loop

Establishing a continuous improvement process involves iteratively refining data quality measures, addressing root causes of data issues, and incorporating feedback from data consumers and stakeholders. Regular reviews, retrospectives, and data quality audits drive ongoing improvements in data quality management practices.

CLI Command for Continuous Improvement and Feedback Loop:
bashCopy code

$ improve-data-quality

10. Data Quality Tools and Platforms

Numerous data quality tools and platforms are available to support organizations in their quest for data quality excellence. These tools offer functionalities such as data profiling, cleansing, validation, monitoring, and governance, empowering data teams to proactively manage and improve data quality.

CLI Command for Data Quality Tools and Platforms:

bashCopy code

```
$ explore-data-quality-tools
```

Ensuring data quality throughout the ETL process is essential for organizations to derive accurate insights and make informed decisions. By implementing robust data quality management practices, leveraging appropriate tools and technologies, and fostering a culture of data stewardship, organizations can enhance the trustworthiness, reliability, and value of their data assets. With a relentless focus on data quality, organizations can unlock the full potential of their data and drive business success in the digital age.

Chapter 10: Emerging Trends in ETL and Data Integration

In the rapidly evolving landscape of data management, ETL (Extract, Transform, Load) and data integration play pivotal roles in ensuring the seamless flow of data across diverse systems and platforms. This chapter explores the latest trends and advancements shaping the ETL and data integration space, from the rise of cloud-native solutions to the emergence of data mesh architectures and the growing importance of real-time data integration.

1. Shift Towards Cloud-Native ETL Solutions

As organizations increasingly embrace cloud computing, there has been a noticeable shift towards cloud-native ETL solutions. These platforms leverage the scalability, flexibility, and cost-effectiveness of cloud infrastructure to handle large volumes of data and complex integration scenarios. Cloud-based ETL tools such as AWS Glue, Google Dataflow, and Azure Data Factory offer built-in connectors, serverless processing, and seamless integration with cloud data sources and services.

CLI Command for Shift Towards Cloud-Native ETL Solutions:

bashCopy code

```
$ deploy-cloud-etl
```

2. Adoption of Modern Data Integration Architectures

Traditional ETL approaches are giving way to more modern and agile data integration architectures. One such approach gaining traction is the data mesh architecture, which advocates for decentralized data ownership, domain-driven data products, and self-serve data infrastructure. By decentralizing data processing and governance responsibilities, data mesh architectures aim to empower domain experts and foster a culture of data-driven decision-making.

CLI Command for Adoption of Modern Data Integration Architectures:

bashCopy code

$ implement-data-mesh

3. Real-Time Data Integration and Streaming Analytics

The demand for real-time insights is driving the adoption of real-time data integration and streaming analytics technologies. Organizations seek to harness the value of data as it is generated, enabling immediate decision-making and actionable insights. Stream processing frameworks such as Apache Kafka, Apache Flink, and Confluent provide the infrastructure needed to ingest, process, and analyze continuous streams of data in real-time.

CLI Command for Real-Time Data Integration and Streaming Analytics:

bashCopy code

$ deploy-streaming-analytics

4. Hybrid Data Integration Approaches

Many organizations operate in hybrid environments, with data distributed across on-premises systems, cloud platforms, and edge devices. Hybrid data integration approaches aim to seamlessly integrate data from disparate sources, regardless of their location or format. Hybrid integration platforms offer connectors for both on-premises and cloud-based systems, along with data synchronization, replication, and orchestration capabilities.

CLI Command for Hybrid Data Integration Approaches:

```bash
bashCopy code
$ configure-hybrid-integration
```

5. Self-Service Data Integration and DataOps

Self-service data integration tools empower business users and data analysts to access, prepare, and integrate data without relying on IT or data engineering teams. These tools offer intuitive interfaces, drag-and-drop functionality, and pre-built connectors, enabling users to quickly create data pipelines and workflows. The adoption of DataOps practices further streamlines the data integration process, promoting collaboration, automation, and continuous delivery of data pipelines.

CLI Command for Self-Service Data Integration and DataOps:

```bash
bashCopy code
$ enable-self-service-integration
```

6. Data Governance and Compliance

With the increasing focus on data privacy, security, and compliance, data governance has become a critical aspect of data integration initiatives. Organizations are investing in data governance frameworks and tools to ensure data quality, integrity, and regulatory compliance throughout the data integration lifecycle. This includes implementing data lineage tracking, access controls, encryption, and audit trails to safeguard sensitive data and mitigate risks.

CLI Command for Data Governance and Compliance:

```bash
bashCopy code
$ enforce-data-governance
```

7. Machine Learning and AI-Powered Integration

Machine learning and artificial intelligence are being leveraged to automate and optimize various aspects of the data integration process. AI-powered integration platforms can automatically discover data relationships, recommend data mappings, detect anomalies, and optimize data flows for better performance and efficiency. By harnessing the power of AI, organizations can accelerate data integration tasks and improve overall productivity.

CLI Command for Machine Learning and AI-Powered Integration:

bashCopy code

$ implement-ai-integration

The landscape of ETL and data integration is undergoing rapid transformation, driven by technological advancements, evolving business requirements, and shifting data paradigms. By embracing cloud-native solutions, modern data integration architectures, real-time processing capabilities, and self-service tools, organizations can unlock the full potential of their data assets and gain a competitive edge in today's data-driven economy. With a strategic approach to data integration, organizations can adapt to changing business needs, leverage emerging technologies, and capitalize on new opportunities for innovation and growth.

Future Directions and Innovations in ETL Technology

As the volume, variety, and velocity of data continue to grow exponentially, the field of Extract, Transform, Load (ETL) technology is undergoing rapid evolution. This chapter explores the emerging trends, future directions, and innovative technologies shaping the future of ETL.

1. Data Integration Platforms

Traditional ETL tools are evolving into comprehensive data integration platforms that offer end-to-end capabilities for data ingestion, transformation, orchestration, and delivery. These platforms leverage advanced technologies such as artificial intelligence (AI), machine learning (ML), and natural language processing (NLP) to automate data integration tasks, optimize performance, and enhance usability. Organizations are increasingly investing in modern data integration platforms to streamline their data pipelines, improve data quality, and accelerate time-to-insight.

CLI Command for Deploying Data Integration Platforms:
bashCopy code

```
$ deploy-data-integration-platform
```

2. Real-Time Data Integration

The demand for real-time analytics is driving the adoption of real-time data integration solutions. Traditional batch-oriented ETL processes are being replaced by stream processing frameworks such as Apache Kafka, Apache Flink, and Confluent, which enable the processing of data in motion. Real-time data integration allows organizations to capture, process, and analyze data as it is generated, enabling faster decision-making, proactive insights, and improved operational efficiency.

CLI Command for Real-Time Data Integration:
bashCopy code

```
$ implement-real-time-etl
```

3. Data Mesh Architecture

The concept of data mesh is gaining traction as organizations seek to democratize data access and promote data-driven decision-making. Unlike traditional centralized data warehouses, data mesh architecture advocates for decentralized data ownership, domain-driven data products, and self-serve data infrastructure.

By empowering domain experts to manage and govern their own data, data mesh architecture promotes agility, innovation, and collaboration across the organization.

CLI Command for Implementing Data Mesh Architecture:

bashCopy code

$ deploy-data-mesh

4. DataOps and Continuous Integration/Continuous Deployment (CI/CD)

DataOps practices are reshaping the way organizations manage and deploy their data pipelines. Similar to DevOps principles, DataOps emphasizes collaboration, automation, and continuous delivery in the data integration process. By implementing CI/CD pipelines for ETL workflows, organizations can accelerate development cycles, improve code quality, and ensure the reliability and repeatability of their data pipelines.

CLI Command for Implementing DataOps:

bashCopy code

$ enable-dataops

5. Data Catalogs and Metadata Management

Data catalogs and metadata management tools are becoming indispensable in modern data integration environments. These platforms provide centralized repositories for metadata, data lineage, and data dictionaries, enabling users to discover, understand, and govern their data assets effectively. By maintaining comprehensive metadata catalogs, organizations can improve data governance, enhance data quality, and ensure compliance with regulatory requirements.

CLI Command for Deploying Data Catalogs:

bashCopy code

$ deploy-data-catalog

6. Data Governance and Compliance

As data privacy regulations become more stringent, organizations are prioritizing data governance and compliance in their ETL processes. Data governance frameworks and tools help organizations establish policies, procedures, and controls to ensure data integrity, security, and privacy. By implementing robust data governance practices, organizations can mitigate risks, build trust with stakeholders, and demonstrate compliance with regulatory requirements.

CLI Command for Implementing Data Governance:

bashCopy code

```
$ enforce-data-governance
```

7. Cloud-Native ETL

The shift towards cloud computing is driving the adoption of cloud-native ETL solutions. Cloud-based ETL platforms offer scalability, flexibility, and cost-effectiveness, allowing organizations to process large volumes of data in a distributed and elastic manner. By leveraging cloud infrastructure and services, organizations can eliminate the need for upfront investments in hardware and software, reduce operational overhead, and focus on innovation and value creation.

CLI Command for Deploying Cloud-Native ETL:

bashCopy code

```
$ deploy-cloud-etl
```

The future of ETL technology is characterized by innovation, automation, and agility. By embracing emerging trends such as real-time data integration, data mesh architecture, DataOps practices, and cloud-native solutions, organizations can unlock new opportunities for data-driven innovation and competitive advantage. With a strategic approach to ETL technology, organizations can adapt to evolving business requirements, harness the power of data, and drive digital transformation in the modern era of data-driven decision-making.

BOOK 4
BIG DATA ANALYTICS
HARNESSING THE POWER OF DATA WAREHOUSING FOR EXPERTS

ROB BOTWRIGHT

Chapter 1: Introduction to Big Data Analytics and Data Warehousing Integration

Big data analytics has emerged as a transformative force in the modern business landscape, enabling organizations to extract valuable insights from vast and diverse datasets. Next, we delve into the fundamentals of big data analytics, its applications, techniques, and the tools used to harness the power of big data.

1. Introduction to Big Data Analytics

Big data analytics refers to the process of examining large and complex datasets to uncover hidden patterns, correlations, and trends that can inform business decisions and drive strategic initiatives. Unlike traditional analytics methods, which are often limited by the size and structure of the data, big data analytics leverages advanced technologies and algorithms to process and analyze massive volumes of data quickly and efficiently.

CLI Command for Deploying Big Data Analytics Tools:

bashCopy code

```
$ deploy-big-data-analytics
```

2. Applications of Big Data Analytics

Big data analytics has diverse applications across various industries, including retail, healthcare, finance, manufacturing, and telecommunications. Organizations use big data analytics to gain insights into customer behavior, optimize operations, detect fraud, improve healthcare outcomes, enhance product development, and drive innovation. By leveraging big data analytics, organizations can gain a competitive edge, identify new opportunities, and mitigate risks more effectively.

CLI Command for Implementing Big Data Analytics Applications:

bashCopy code

$ implement-big-data-analytics-apps

3. Techniques in Big Data Analytics

Big data analytics encompasses a wide range of techniques and methodologies, including descriptive analytics, diagnostic analytics, predictive analytics, and prescriptive analytics. Descriptive analytics focuses on summarizing historical data to understand what has happened in the past. Diagnostic analytics aims to identify the root causes of events or patterns. Predictive analytics leverages statistical models and machine learning algorithms to forecast future outcomes. Prescriptive analytics provides recommendations on the best course of action to achieve desired outcomes.

CLI Command for Executing Big Data Analytics Techniques:

bashCopy code

$ execute-big-data-analytics-techniques

4. Tools for Big Data Analytics

A variety of tools and technologies are available for conducting big data analytics, ranging from open-source platforms like Apache Hadoop, Apache Spark, and Apache Flink to commercial solutions like Microsoft Azure, Google BigQuery, and Amazon Redshift. These tools offer capabilities for data ingestion, storage, processing, analysis, and visualization, allowing organizations to build end-to-end big data analytics pipelines tailored to their specific needs and requirements.

CLI Command for Selecting and Configuring Big Data Analytics Tools:

bashCopy code

$ configure-big-data-analytics-tools

5. Challenges in Big Data Analytics

While big data analytics offers significant opportunities, it also presents various challenges, including data quality issues, scalability concerns, privacy and security risks, and the complexity of integrating diverse data sources. Organizations must address these challenges by implementing robust data governance practices, ensuring data quality and integrity, adopting scalable infrastructure and technologies, and complying with regulatory requirements to realize the full potential of big data analytics.

CLI Command for Addressing Challenges in Big Data Analytics:

bashCopy code

$ address-big-data-analytics-challenges

6. Future Trends in Big Data Analytics

The field of big data analytics continues to evolve rapidly, driven by advancements in technology, the proliferation of data sources, and changing business needs. Future trends in big data analytics include the integration of artificial intelligence (AI) and machine learning (ML) techniques, the rise of edge computing and real-time analytics, the adoption of cloud-native architectures, and the growing emphasis on responsible AI and ethical data usage. By staying abreast of these trends, organizations can leverage the latest innovations in big data analytics to gain a competitive advantage and drive digital transformation.

CLI Command for Staying Updated on Big Data Analytics Trends:

bashCopy code

$ monitor-big-data-analytics-trends

Big data analytics is revolutionizing how organizations derive insights, make decisions, and drive innovation in today's data-driven world. By understanding the fundamentals of big data analytics, exploring its applications and techniques, leveraging the right tools and technologies, addressing challenges, and embracing future trends, organizations can unlock the full potential of big data analytics to achieve their business objectives and stay ahead in a rapidly evolving landscape.

Integration Challenges and Opportunities

In the dynamic landscape of data warehousing and analytics, integration plays a crucial role in ensuring the seamless flow of data across systems, applications, and platforms. This chapter explores the challenges and opportunities associated with data integration, highlighting key strategies and techniques for overcoming integration hurdles and maximizing the benefits of interconnected data environments.

1. Understanding Integration Challenges

Data integration involves combining data from disparate sources, formats, and structures to provide a unified view of information for analysis and decision-making. However, organizations often face several challenges in achieving effective data integration. These challenges include data silos, where data is stored in isolated systems, incompatible data formats and schemas, varying data quality standards, and the complexity of integrating legacy systems with modern technologies. Addressing these challenges requires careful planning, robust data governance practices, and the adoption of flexible integration architectures.

CLI Command for Identifying Integration Challenges:

bashCopy code

```
$ identify-integration-challenges
```

2. Data Integration Strategies

To overcome integration challenges, organizations can employ various data integration strategies, including batch processing, real-time data integration, and hybrid approaches. Batch processing involves collecting and processing data in predefined intervals, making it suitable for scenarios where near real-time data processing is not required. Real-time data integration, on the other hand, enables organizations to process and analyze data as it arrives, providing timely insights for decision-making. Hybrid approaches combine batch and real-time processing to achieve a balance between speed and scalability, depending on specific business requirements.

CLI Command for Implementing Data Integration Strategies:

bashCopy code

$ implement-data-integration-strategies

3. ETL vs. ELT

Two common approaches to data integration are Extract, Transform, Load (ETL) and Extract, Load, Transform (ELT). In the traditional ETL approach, data is extracted from source systems, transformed into the desired format, and then loaded into the target data warehouse. In contrast, the ELT approach involves extracting data first, loading it into the target system, and then performing transformations within the data warehouse itself. While ETL is suitable for scenarios requiring extensive data cleansing and transformation, ELT offers advantages in terms of scalability, performance, and flexibility.

CLI Command for Choosing Between ETL and ELT:

bashCopy code

$ select-etl-or-elt

4. Data Governance and Security Considerations

Effective data integration requires robust data governance and security measures to ensure the confidentiality, integrity, and availability of data throughout the integration process. Organizations must establish clear policies and procedures for data access, usage, and sharing, implement encryption and authentication mechanisms to protect sensitive information, and adhere to regulatory compliance requirements such as GDPR, HIPAA, and CCPA. By prioritizing data governance and security, organizations can mitigate risks and build trust in their integrated data environments.

CLI Command for Implementing Data Governance and Security Measures:

bashCopy code

$ implement-data-governance-and-security

5. Integration Platforms and Technologies

A wide range of integration platforms and technologies are available to streamline data integration processes and enhance interoperability between systems. These include enterprise service buses (ESBs), data integration tools, application programming interfaces (APIs), and cloud-based integration platforms. Organizations can leverage these technologies to automate data workflows, orchestrate data movements, and integrate data across on-premises and cloud environments seamlessly. Choosing the right integration platform depends on factors such as scalability, flexibility, ease of use, and compatibility with existing systems.

CLI Command for Selecting Integration Platforms and Technologies:

bashCopy code

$ choose-integration-platform

6. Opportunities for Innovation

While integration challenges abound, they also present opportunities for innovation and optimization. By embracing emerging technologies such as artificial intelligence (AI), machine learning (ML), and robotic process automation (RPA), organizations can automate repetitive integration tasks, improve data quality and accuracy, and unlock new insights from integrated data sources. Additionally, advancements in data virtualization, distributed computing, and containerization offer novel approaches to data integration, enabling organizations to build agile, scalable, and resilient data architectures.

CLI Command for Exploring Innovative Integration Technologies:

bashCopy code

```
$ explore-innovative-integration-tech
```

In today's data-driven world, effective data integration is essential for organizations seeking to derive insights, make informed decisions, and drive innovation. By understanding the challenges and opportunities associated with data integration, implementing appropriate strategies and technologies, and prioritizing data governance and security, organizations can build robust, interconnected data ecosystems that support their business objectives and drive competitive advantage in a rapidly evolving digital landscape.

Chapter 2: Advanced Data Warehousing Architectures for Big Data

In the era of big data, organizations are grappling with vast volumes of data generated at unprecedented velocities from various sources such as social media, IoT devices, and business applications. To harness the potential of big data for analytics and decision-making, it's essential to design robust data warehousing architectures that can accommodate the scale, complexity, and diversity of big data sources. This chapter explores the architectural considerations for big data warehousing, focusing on key principles, design patterns, and technologies to build scalable and efficient data platforms.

1. Scalability and Elasticity

Scalability is a critical consideration in big data warehousing architectures to accommodate the ever-growing volume of data and user demands. Traditional relational database systems may struggle to handle the scale of big data, leading to performance bottlenecks and scalability limitations. To address this challenge, organizations adopt distributed data processing frameworks such as Apache Hadoop and Apache Spark, which enable horizontal scalability by distributing data and computation across multiple nodes in a cluster. Additionally, cloud-based data warehousing solutions such as Amazon Redshift, Google BigQuery, and Azure Synapse Analytics offer elastic scalability, allowing organizations to dynamically scale resources up or down based on workload demands.

CLI Command for Scaling Resources in Cloud-Based Data Warehousing:

bashCopy code

```
$       scale-cloud-data-warehouse       --instance-type=<instance_type> --nodes=<num_nodes>
```

2. Data Storage and Management

Effective management of big data requires efficient storage solutions capable of storing and processing diverse data types, including structured, semi-structured, and unstructured data. Traditional relational databases may not be suitable for storing unstructured data such as text, images, and videos. Organizations leverage distributed file systems like Hadoop Distributed File System (HDFS) and object storage systems such as Amazon S3 and Azure Blob Storage for storing and managing big data. These storage systems provide scalability, fault tolerance, and cost-effectiveness, making them ideal choices for big data warehousing architectures.

CLI Command for Managing Data Storage in HDFS:

bashCopy code

```
$ hdfs dfs - mkdir /data
```

3. Data Ingestion and Processing

In big data warehousing architectures, efficient data ingestion and processing pipelines are essential for collecting, transforming, and loading data into the data warehouse. Apache Kafka, Apache NiFi, and Amazon Kinesis are popular streaming data platforms used for real-time data ingestion from various sources. These platforms enable organizations to capture and process data streams in real-time, providing timely insights for decision-making. Additionally, data processing frameworks like Apache Spark and Apache Flink facilitate batch and stream processing, enabling organizations to perform complex analytics on large datasets.

CLI Command for Starting Apache Kafka Service:

bashCopy code

```
$ kafka-server-start.sh config/server.properties
```

4. Data Governance and Security

Ensuring data governance and security is paramount in big data warehousing architectures to protect sensitive information, comply with regulatory requirements, and maintain data integrity and privacy. Organizations implement robust data governance frameworks and access control mechanisms to govern data usage, enforce data quality standards, and mitigate risks associated with data breaches and unauthorized access. Encryption, authentication, and authorization technologies are employed to secure data both at rest and in transit, safeguarding it from unauthorized access and malicious attacks.

CLI Command for Configuring Data Encryption:

bashCopy code

```
$ configure-data-encryption --algorithm=AES --key=<encryption_key>
```

5. Metadata Management

Metadata management is crucial in big data warehousing architectures to catalog, organize, and govern metadata assets such as data schemas, data lineage, and data definitions. Metadata management tools and platforms enable organizations to discover, understand, and trace data lineage across the data ecosystem, facilitating data governance, compliance, and data quality initiatives. Apache Atlas, Collibra, and Informatica Metadata Manager are examples of metadata management solutions used to manage metadata in big data environments.

CLI Command for Registering Metadata in Apache Atlas:

bashCopy code

```
$ atlas-metadata-register --type=<metadata_type> --name=<metadata_name>
```

6. Fault Tolerance and High Availability

Maintaining fault tolerance and high availability is essential in big data warehousing architectures to ensure continuous access to data and minimize downtime in the event of failures or disruptions. Distributed data processing frameworks and storage systems incorporate fault tolerance mechanisms such as data replication, data redundancy, and automatic failover to withstand node failures and system outages. Additionally, organizations deploy disaster recovery and backup solutions to protect against data loss and ensure business continuity.

CLI Command for Enabling Automatic Failover in Hadoop:

bashCopy code

```
$ hdfs haadmin -transitionToActive <active_node>
```

Architectural considerations play a crucial role in designing scalable, efficient, and resilient big data warehousing solutions. By addressing scalability, data storage and management, data ingestion and processing, data governance and security, metadata management, and fault tolerance, organizations can build robust data platforms capable of unlocking the full potential of big data for analytics, insights, and innovation in today's data-driven world.

Hybrid Architectures: Merging Traditional and Big Data Approaches

In the realm of data management, organizations often find themselves navigating a complex landscape where traditional relational databases coexist with emerging big data technologies. Hybrid architectures emerge as a strategic solution to leverage the strengths of both traditional and big data approaches, enabling organizations to effectively manage diverse data types, handle large volumes of data, and extract actionable insights. This chapter delves into the concept of hybrid architectures, exploring their benefits, challenges, and best practices in integrating traditional and big data technologies.

1. Understanding Hybrid Architectures

Hybrid architectures blend the best of traditional data management techniques, characterized by structured data models and relational databases, with the scalability and flexibility of big data technologies designed for handling unstructured and semi-structured data at scale. By integrating traditional and big data components, organizations can address a wide range of use cases, from real-time analytics and business intelligence to data warehousing and machine learning.

2. Benefits of Hybrid Architectures

One of the primary benefits of hybrid architectures is their ability to accommodate diverse data sources and workloads. Traditional databases excel in managing structured data with ACID (Atomicity, Consistency, Isolation, Durability) properties, ensuring data integrity and transactional consistency. On the other hand, big data technologies such as Apache Hadoop and Apache Spark offer distributed processing capabilities for handling large-scale data processing and analytics tasks.

3. Deploying a Hybrid Architecture

Deploying a hybrid architecture involves integrating traditional relational databases with big data platforms, often leveraging data integration tools and technologies to facilitate seamless data movement and transformation. Organizations may adopt a phased approach, starting with data ingestion and processing in a big data environment before integrating insights back into traditional databases for reporting and analytics.

CLI Command for Deploying a Hybrid Architecture:

bashCopy code

```
$ deploy-hybrid-architecture --traditional-db=<db_name>
--big-data-platform=<platform_name>
```

4. Challenges of Hybrid Architectures

Despite their benefits, hybrid architectures pose several challenges, including complexity, data integration issues, and skill gaps. Integrating disparate data sources and technologies requires careful planning and coordination, as well as expertise in both traditional and big data domains. Moreover, ensuring data consistency, security, and governance across hybrid environments can be challenging, requiring robust governance frameworks and data management practices.

5. Best Practices for Implementing Hybrid Architectures

To successfully implement hybrid architectures, organizations should adhere to best practices that promote interoperability, scalability, and maintainability. This includes adopting standardized data formats and protocols for seamless data exchange, implementing data governance and security measures to protect sensitive information, and investing in training and skill development to bridge the gap between traditional and big data technologies.

6. Use Cases for Hybrid Architectures

Hybrid architectures find applications across various industries and use cases, including real-time analytics, customer relationship management, fraud detection, and supply chain optimization. For example, retailers can leverage hybrid architectures to combine transactional data from traditional databases with clickstream data from web applications to gain insights into customer behavior and preferences in real-time.

7. Future Trends in Hybrid Architectures

As organizations continue to embrace digital transformation and adopt cloud-native technologies, the evolution of hybrid architectures is expected to accelerate. The emergence of hybrid cloud environments, containerization technologies, and serverless computing models will further blur the lines between traditional and big data approaches, paving the way for more seamless and integrated data management solutions.

Hybrid architectures represent a pragmatic approach to data management, allowing organizations to harness the power of both traditional and big data technologies to meet the evolving demands of modern business environments. By integrating structured and unstructured data, leveraging distributed processing capabilities, and embracing best practices in data governance and security, organizations can unlock new opportunities for innovation and growth in the digital age.

Chapter 3: Scalable Data Storage Solutions for Big Data Warehousing

In the era of big data, organizations face unprecedented challenges in storing, managing, and analyzing massive volumes of data generated from diverse sources. Scalability emerges as a critical requirement for big data storage solutions, enabling organizations to accommodate exponential data growth, support concurrent access by multiple users, and maintain performance and reliability at scale. This chapter explores the scalability requirements for big data storage, discussing various approaches, technologies, and best practices to address the growing demands of data storage in the digital age.

1. Understanding Scalability in Big Data Storage

Scalability refers to the ability of a storage system to handle increasing data volumes, user loads, and processing demands without sacrificing performance or reliability. In the context of big data, scalability encompasses both vertical scalability, which involves adding resources such as CPU, memory, and storage capacity to a single node, and horizontal scalability, which involves distributing data and workload across multiple nodes in a cluster.

2. Key Factors Driving Scalability Requirements

Several factors drive the scalability requirements for big data storage, including data volume, velocity, variety, and veracity. The exponential growth of data from sources such as social media, IoT devices, and enterprise applications necessitates scalable storage solutions capable of handling petabytes or even exabytes of data.

Moreover, the need for real-time or near-real-time analytics requires storage systems to support high-throughput data ingestion and processing at scale.

3. Scaling Techniques for Big Data Storage

To achieve scalability, organizations can employ various scaling techniques, including scale-up and scale-out architectures. Scale-up architectures involve adding more resources to a single server or storage device, such as increasing CPU cores, memory capacity, or storage capacity. Scale-out architectures, on the other hand, distribute data and processing across multiple nodes in a cluster, enabling linear scalability by adding additional nodes as needed.

CLI Command for Scaling Out a Storage Cluster:

bashCopy code

```
$ scale-out-storage-cluster --nodes=<num_nodes> --storage=<storage_type>
```

4. Technologies for Scalable Big Data Storage

Several technologies have emerged to address the scalability requirements of big data storage, including distributed file systems, NoSQL databases, and object storage solutions. Distributed file systems such as Hadoop Distributed File System (HDFS) and Apache HBase provide scalable storage for large-scale data processing and analytics workloads. NoSQL databases like Apache Cassandra and MongoDB offer horizontal scalability and high availability for semi-structured and unstructured data.

5. Cloud-Based Storage Solutions

Cloud computing platforms such as Amazon Web Services (AWS), Microsoft Azure, and Google Cloud Platform (GCP) provide scalable storage services, including object storage, block storage, and managed database services. Organizations can leverage cloud-based storage solutions to elastically scale storage capacity up or down based on demand, without the need for upfront capital investment in hardware infrastructure.

6. Best Practices for Scalable Big Data Storage

Achieving scalable big data storage requires careful planning, architecture design, and implementation. Best practices include data partitioning and sharding to distribute data across multiple nodes, data replication for fault tolerance and high availability, and the use of compression and deduplication techniques to optimize storage efficiency. Additionally, organizations should regularly monitor and tune their storage systems to ensure optimal performance and resource utilization.

7. Challenges and Considerations

While scalable storage solutions offer numerous benefits, they also present challenges such as data consistency, data migration, and operational complexity. Organizations must consider factors such as data governance, security, and compliance requirements when implementing scalable big data storage solutions. Furthermore, choosing the right storage architecture and technology stack requires careful evaluation of factors such as performance, cost, and vendor support.

Scalability is a fundamental requirement for big data storage solutions, enabling organizations to efficiently manage and process vast amounts of data in today's data-driven world. By leveraging scalable storage architectures, technologies, and best practices, organizations can effectively address the challenges of data growth, support evolving business requirements, and unlock the full potential of their data assets for actionable insights and competitive advantage.

Evaluating Scalable Storage Solutions

In the era of big data, organizations are constantly seeking scalable storage solutions to accommodate the exponential growth of data volumes, support diverse workloads, and ensure high performance and reliability. Evaluating scalable storage solutions involves assessing various factors such as scalability, performance, reliability, cost-effectiveness, and ease of management. This chapter explores the key considerations and methodologies for evaluating scalable storage solutions, providing insights into the selection process and guiding organizations towards making informed decisions that align with their business objectives and requirements.

1. Understanding Scalability in Storage Solutions

Scalability is a critical factor in evaluating storage solutions, as it determines the system's ability to handle increasing data volumes, user loads, and processing demands without compromising performance or reliability. Scalability can be evaluated based on both vertical scalability, which involves adding resources to a single node, and horizontal scalability, which involves distributing data and workload across multiple nodes in a cluster.

2. Performance Metrics and Benchmarks

Performance is another crucial aspect of storage solution evaluation, as it directly impacts the system's ability to meet workload requirements and deliver timely insights. Performance metrics such as throughput, latency, IOPS

(Input/Output Operations Per Second), and response time should be carefully evaluated under various workload conditions and scenarios. Benchmarking tools and methodologies can help organizations assess the performance of different storage solutions and identify the most suitable option for their specific use cases.

CLI Command for Benchmarking Storage Performance:

bashCopy code

```
$ storage-benchmark --type=<benchmark_type> --workload=<workload_profile> --duration=<test_duration>
```

3. Reliability and Data Integrity

Reliability and data integrity are paramount considerations when evaluating storage solutions, especially for mission-critical applications and sensitive data. Organizations should assess factors such as data redundancy, fault tolerance mechanisms, data protection features (e.g., RAID configurations, checksums), and disaster recovery capabilities to ensure the integrity and availability of their data assets.

4. Cost-Effectiveness and Total Cost of Ownership (TCO)

Cost-effectiveness is a key criterion in storage solution evaluation, as organizations strive to maximize ROI (Return on Investment) while minimizing capital and operational expenses. In addition to upfront acquisition costs, organizations should consider factors such as scalability, maintenance, energy consumption, and licensing fees when calculating the total cost of ownership (TCO) for different storage solutions over their lifecycle.

CLI Command for Calculating TCO:

bashCopy code

```
$ calculate-tco --solution=<storage_solution> --
duration=<lifecycle_duration> --
cost_components=<cost_factors>
```

5. Management and Administration

Ease of management and administration is essential for efficient operation and maintenance of storage solutions, especially in large-scale deployments. Organizations should evaluate management features such as centralized monitoring and management consoles, automation capabilities, APIs (Application Programming Interfaces) for integration with existing tools and workflows, and support for configuration management and policy-based administration.

6. Scalability and Growth Potential

Scalability is a fundamental requirement for modern storage solutions, allowing organizations to seamlessly accommodate data growth and evolving business requirements. When evaluating storage solutions, organizations should assess scalability aspects such as storage capacity expansion, performance scaling, support for heterogeneous environments, and compatibility with emerging technologies and standards.

7. Vendor Support and Ecosystem

Vendor support and ecosystem play a crucial role in the success of storage solution deployments, as organizations rely on vendors for technical support, software updates, patches, and training. Organizations should evaluate vendors based on factors such as reputation, track record, service level agreements (SLAs), support channels, and the availability of certified consultants and integration partners.

8. Security and Compliance Considerations

Security and compliance are paramount concerns in storage solution evaluation, especially in industries subject to regulatory requirements such as healthcare, finance, and government. Organizations should assess security features such as encryption, access controls, authentication mechanisms, audit logging, and compliance certifications (e.g., HIPAA, GDPR) to ensure the protection and privacy of sensitive data.

Evaluating scalable storage solutions is a complex and multifaceted process that requires careful consideration of various factors such as scalability, performance, reliability, cost-effectiveness, management, security, and compliance. By adopting a systematic approach to evaluation, leveraging benchmarking tools and methodologies, and prioritizing their specific business requirements and objectives, organizations can make informed decisions and select the most suitable storage solution to meet their current and future needs.

Chapter 4: Parallel Processing and Distributed Computing for Big Data

Parallel processing is a fundamental concept in computing that involves the simultaneous execution of multiple tasks or instructions to achieve faster and more efficient computation. It plays a crucial role in various computing domains, including data processing, scientific simulations, and artificial intelligence. This chapter explores the key concepts and techniques of parallel processing, providing insights into its principles, applications, and deployment strategies.

1. Understanding Parallel Processing

Parallel processing refers to the execution of multiple tasks or instructions concurrently, allowing for increased throughput, reduced latency, and improved performance compared to sequential processing. In parallel processing systems, tasks are divided into smaller subtasks, which are then executed simultaneously on multiple processing units or cores.

2. Types of Parallelism

Parallel processing can be categorized into different types based on the level of granularity and the degree of concurrency:

Task Parallelism: Involves parallelizing independent tasks or operations across multiple processing units.

Data Parallelism: Involves parallelizing operations on data elements or segments by distributing data across multiple processing units.

Instruction-level Parallelism: Involves parallelizing individual instructions within a single task or program to exploit concurrency at the instruction level.

3. Parallel Processing Architectures

Parallel processing architectures can vary in terms of their organization, interconnect topology, and memory hierarchy. Common parallel processing architectures include:

Shared-memory Architectures: Feature a single, globally shared memory space accessible by all processing units, enabling communication and synchronization through shared variables or locks.

Distributed-memory Architectures: Feature multiple independent memory modules associated with individual processing units, requiring explicit message passing for communication and synchronization.

Hybrid Architectures: Combine elements of both shared-memory and distributed-memory architectures to leverage the benefits of each approach.

4. Parallel Processing Models

Parallel processing models define the structure and behavior of parallel programs, including how tasks are decomposed, how data is distributed, and how communication and synchronization are managed. Common parallel processing models include:

Task-based Models: Represent parallel programs as a collection of independent tasks or threads that can execute concurrently and communicate through shared data structures or message passing.

Dataflow Models: Represent parallel programs as directed graphs of data dependencies, where tasks are triggered based on the availability of input data and execute asynchronously as data becomes available.

Message Passing Models: Represent parallel programs as a collection of processes or actors that communicate exclusively through message passing primitives, such as send and receive operations.

5. Parallel Processing Paradigms

Parallel processing paradigms refer to high-level programming constructs and patterns used to express parallelism in applications. Common parallel processing paradigms include:

MapReduce: A programming model for processing large-scale datasets in parallel across distributed computing clusters, comprising two main phases: map, which applies a function to each input record and emits intermediate key-value pairs, and reduce, which aggregates and processes intermediate key-value pairs.

Bulk Synchronous Parallel (BSP): A parallel programming model based on the synchronization of computation and communication in supersteps, where tasks execute concurrently within a superstep and synchronize their state at the end of each superstep.

Fork-Join: A parallel programming pattern that involves dividing a task into subtasks (forking) and then combining the results of subtasks (joining) to produce the final result.

6. Deployment Strategies for Parallel Processing

Deploying parallel processing applications involves selecting appropriate hardware, software, and programming models based on the specific requirements and characteristics of the application. Common deployment strategies include:

Task Partitioning: Decomposing tasks or datasets into smaller units and distributing them across processing units or nodes based on workload characteristics and resource availability.

Load Balancing: Ensuring equitable distribution of computational workload among processing units or nodes to maximize resource utilization and minimize idle time.

Data Partitioning: Distributing data across processing units or nodes based on data access patterns, data dependencies, and communication overheads to minimize data movement and improve locality.

Parallel processing is a powerful computing paradigm that enables faster and more efficient execution of computational tasks by leveraging concurrency and parallelism. By understanding the principles, architectures, models, paradigms, and deployment strategies of parallel processing, organizations can design and deploy scalable, high-performance parallel processing applications to address a wide range of computational challenges and accelerate innovation in various domains.

Distributed computing frameworks have revolutionized the way big data is processed and analyzed, enabling organizations to tackle large-scale data processing challenges efficiently and effectively. These frameworks provide the infrastructure and tools necessary to distribute data processing tasks across multiple nodes in a cluster, allowing for parallel execution and scalable performance. Next, we explore several prominent distributed computing frameworks for big data processing, including Apache Hadoop, Apache Spark, and Apache

Flink, discussing their features, architecture, and use cases.

1. Apache Hadoop

Apache Hadoop is one of the most widely adopted distributed computing frameworks for big data processing. It consists of two core components: the Hadoop Distributed File System (HDFS) for distributed storage and the MapReduce programming model for distributed processing. Hadoop utilizes a master-slave architecture, with a single NameNode responsible for managing the file system namespace and multiple DataNodes storing data in a distributed manner across the cluster.

To deploy Apache Hadoop, users can download the distribution package from the official Apache Hadoop website and follow the installation instructions provided in the documentation. Once installed, users can interact with Hadoop using various command-line tools, such as **hadoop fs** for managing files in HDFS and **hadoop jar** for submitting MapReduce jobs.

2. Apache Spark

Apache Spark is a powerful distributed computing framework designed for in-memory data processing and iterative algorithms. Unlike Hadoop MapReduce, which relies on disk-based storage and intermediate data shuffle, Spark leverages in-memory computing and resilient distributed datasets (RDDs) to achieve high performance and fault tolerance. Spark provides a rich set of APIs in Scala, Java, Python, and R, making it accessible to a wide range of developers.

To deploy Apache Spark, users can download the Spark distribution package from the official Apache Spark website and follow the installation instructions provided in the documentation. Spark supports various deployment modes, including standalone mode, YARN mode, and Mesos mode, allowing users to choose the deployment option that best suits their infrastructure and requirements. Once installed, users can interact with Spark using the Spark shell or submit Spark applications using the **spark-submit** command-line tool.

3. Apache Flink

Apache Flink is a stream processing framework with native support for event time processing, stateful computations, and exactly-once semantics. Flink's architecture is based on a distributed streaming dataflow engine, which allows for low-latency, high-throughput processing of real-time data streams. Flink provides APIs in Java and Scala for building streaming and batch processing applications, as well as support for SQL queries and complex event processing (CEP).

To deploy Apache Flink, users can download the Flink distribution package from the official Apache Flink website and follow the installation instructions provided in the documentation. Flink supports various deployment modes, including standalone mode, YARN mode, and Kubernetes mode, enabling users to deploy Flink on different cluster management systems. Once installed, users can interact with Flink using the Flink command-line interface (CLI) and submit Flink jobs using the **flink run** command.

4. Use Cases and Applications

Distributed computing frameworks like Hadoop, Spark, and Flink are used in a wide range of applications and use cases, including:

Large-scale data processing: Analyzing vast amounts of structured and unstructured data to extract valuable insights and patterns.

Real-time analytics: Processing and analyzing streaming data from sources such as IoT devices, social media, and financial transactions in real-time.

Machine learning and AI: Training and deploying machine learning models at scale using distributed computing resources.

ETL and data integration: Extracting, transforming, and loading data from various sources into a centralized data warehouse or data lake.

Distributed computing frameworks play a critical role in enabling organizations to process and analyze big data efficiently and effectively. By leveraging frameworks like Apache Hadoop, Apache Spark, and Apache Flink, organizations can tackle large-scale data processing challenges, unlock valuable insights from their data, and drive innovation in various domains.

Chapter 5: Advanced Analytics Techniques: Machine Learning and Predictive Modeling

Machine learning algorithms have become indispensable tools in the realm of big data analytics, enabling organizations to derive valuable insights and make data-driven decisions at scale. Next, we will delve into various machine learning algorithms tailored for big data analytics, discussing their principles, applications, and deployment strategies.

1. Linear Regression

Linear regression is a fundamental supervised learning algorithm used for modeling the relationship between a dependent variable and one or more independent variables. In the context of big data analytics, linear regression can be applied to predict continuous outcomes based on input features. It is particularly useful for tasks such as sales forecasting, risk assessment, and demand prediction.

To deploy linear regression on big data, organizations can leverage distributed computing frameworks like Apache Spark or Apache Flink. Using the **spark.ml** library in Spark or the **flink-ml** library in Flink, users can train linear regression models on large datasets and make predictions at scale.

2. Logistic Regression

Logistic regression is another widely used supervised learning algorithm for binary classification tasks. It models the probability that a given instance belongs to a particular class based on its features. Logistic regression is commonly used in applications such as spam detection, churn prediction, and fraud detection.

Similar to linear regression, logistic regression can be deployed on big data using distributed computing frameworks like Spark or Flink. By leveraging the respective machine learning libraries, organizations can train logistic regression models on large datasets and deploy them in production environments for real-time classification.

3. Decision Trees and Random Forests

Decision trees are versatile supervised learning algorithms that partition the feature space into hierarchical decision nodes, making them suitable for both classification and regression tasks. Random forests extend the concept of decision trees by aggregating multiple trees to improve predictive accuracy and reduce overfitting.

To deploy decision trees and random forests on big data, organizations can utilize scalable implementations available in libraries such as Apache Spark's **spark.ml** or Apache Flink's **flink-ml**. By distributing the training process across a cluster of machines, these frameworks enable efficient processing of large datasets and the construction of complex ensemble models.

4. Support Vector Machines (SVM)

Support vector machines (SVM) are powerful supervised learning algorithms used for classification and regression tasks. SVMs aim to find the optimal hyperplane that separates data points belonging to different classes while maximizing the margin between classes. SVMs are effective for tasks such as image classification, text categorization, and anomaly detection.

To deploy SVMs on big data, organizations can leverage scalable implementations available in machine learning libraries compatible with distributed computing frameworks. By parallelizing the computation of SVM models across multiple nodes in a cluster, organizations can train models on massive datasets and achieve high predictive accuracy.

5. Neural Networks

Neural networks, particularly deep learning models, have gained prominence in recent years for their ability to learn complex patterns from large volumes of data. Deep learning architectures such as convolutional neural networks (CNNs) and recurrent neural networks (RNNs) are widely used in image recognition, natural language processing, and time series analysis.

Deploying neural networks for big data analytics requires specialized frameworks optimized for distributed training. Apache Spark provides support for deep learning through libraries like TensorFlowOnSpark and BigDL, while Apache Flink offers the capability to train neural networks using its built-in machine learning APIs.

Machine learning algorithms are essential tools for extracting insights and value from big data. By leveraging distributed computing frameworks and scalable machine learning libraries, organizations can deploy a wide range of algorithms to tackle diverse analytics tasks at scale. From linear regression and logistic regression to decision trees, support vector machines, and neural networks, the arsenal of machine learning algorithms available for big data analytics continues to expand, empowering organizations to unlock the full potential of their data assets.

Predictive modeling is a powerful technique used across various industries to forecast future outcomes based on historical data. Next, we will explore predictive modeling strategies and their applications, covering techniques, tools, and best practices for deploying predictive models effectively.

1. Understanding Predictive Modeling

Predictive modeling involves building mathematical models that leverage historical data to predict future events or outcomes. These models analyze patterns and relationships within the data to make predictions, enabling organizations to anticipate trends, mitigate risks, and make informed decisions. Predictive modeling is applied across diverse domains, including finance, marketing, healthcare, and manufacturing, to address various predictive tasks such as classification, regression, and clustering.

2. Types of Predictive Modeling Techniques

a. Regression Analysis: Regression models are used to predict continuous numerical outcomes based on input features. Techniques such as linear regression, polynomial regression, and ridge regression are commonly employed for predictive modeling tasks where the target variable is continuous.

b. Classification Algorithms: Classification models are utilized to predict categorical outcomes or assign labels to data points based on their features. Popular classification algorithms include logistic regression, decision trees, random forests, support vector machines (SVM), and neural networks.

c. Time Series Forecasting: Time series forecasting involves predicting future values of a time-dependent variable based on its past values. Techniques such as autoregressive integrated moving average (ARIMA), exponential smoothing methods, and recurrent neural networks (RNNs) are commonly used for time series prediction tasks.

d. Ensemble Methods: Ensemble methods combine multiple base models to improve predictive performance and reduce overfitting. Techniques such as bagging, boosting, and stacking are widely employed to build robust predictive models by aggregating the predictions of multiple models.

3. Tools and Technologies for Predictive Modeling

a. Python Libraries: Python offers a rich ecosystem of libraries for predictive modeling, including scikit-learn,

TensorFlow, Keras, XGBoost, and LightGBM. These libraries provide comprehensive support for various machine learning algorithms and enable efficient model development, training, and evaluation.

b. R Programming: R is another popular language for predictive modeling, with packages such as caret, randomForest, glmnet, and forecast offering extensive functionality for building predictive models. R's rich statistical capabilities make it well-suited for exploratory data analysis and model interpretation.

c. Data Science Platforms: Data science platforms such as IBM Watson Studio, Microsoft Azure Machine Learning, and Databricks provide integrated environments for end-to-end predictive modeling workflows. These platforms offer features for data preparation, model development, deployment, and monitoring, streamlining the entire predictive modeling process.

4. Best Practices for Deploying Predictive Models

a. Data Preparation: High-quality data is essential for building accurate predictive models. Proper data preprocessing steps, including data cleaning, feature engineering, and normalization, should be performed to ensure the reliability and validity of the predictive models.

b. Model Selection: It is crucial to select the most appropriate predictive modeling technique based on the nature of the data and the predictive task at hand. Comparative evaluation of multiple algorithms using cross-validation techniques can help identify the best-performing model for deployment.

c. Model Evaluation: Predictive models should be evaluated using appropriate performance metrics such as accuracy, precision, recall, F1-score, and area under the ROC curve (AUC). Model evaluation should be conducted on separate validation datasets to assess generalization performance and avoid overfitting.

d. Model Deployment: Once a predictive model has been trained and evaluated, it needs to be deployed into production environments for real-world usage. Model deployment involves integrating the model into existing systems, implementing monitoring mechanisms, and ensuring scalability and reliability.

5. Applications of Predictive Modeling

a. Financial Forecasting: Predictive modeling is used in finance for tasks such as stock price prediction, risk assessment, credit scoring, and fraud detection. Banks and financial institutions leverage predictive models to identify potential risks and opportunities and make data-driven decisions.

b. Marketing Analytics: Predictive modeling plays a crucial role in marketing analytics for customer segmentation, churn prediction, recommendation systems, and campaign optimization. By analyzing historical customer data, organizations can target the right audience with personalized marketing strategies.

c. Healthcare Predictive Analytics: In healthcare, predictive modeling is applied for disease prediction, patient diagnosis, treatment recommendation, and hospital resource optimization. Predictive models help healthcare providers improve patient outcomes, reduce costs, and enhance operational efficiency.

d. Supply Chain Optimization: Predictive modeling is used in supply chain management for demand forecasting, inventory optimization, and logistics planning. By accurately predicting demand and supply patterns, organizations can optimize inventory levels, reduce stockouts, and minimize transportation costs.

Predictive modeling is a versatile technique with numerous applications across industries, enabling organizations to extract valuable insights from data and make informed decisions. By leveraging advanced machine learning algorithms, tools, and best practices, organizations can build accurate predictive models that drive business value and competitive advantage. From financial forecasting and marketing analytics to healthcare predictive analytics and supply chain optimization, predictive modeling empowers organizations to anticipate trends, mitigate risks, and capitalize on opportunities in an increasingly data-driven world.

Chapter 6: Real-Time Data Processing and Streaming Analytics

Real-time data processing has become increasingly important in today's fast-paced digital world, enabling organizations to gain instant insights from streaming data sources and respond rapidly to changing conditions. However, real-time data processing comes with its own set of challenges, including scalability, latency, data quality, and fault tolerance. Next, we will explore these challenges and discuss various solutions to address them effectively.

1. Scalability Challenges

Real-time data processing systems must be able to handle large volumes of data efficiently to meet the demands of growing data streams. As data volumes increase, traditional architectures may struggle to scale horizontally to accommodate the additional load. To address scalability challenges, organizations can adopt distributed data processing frameworks such as Apache Kafka, Apache Flink, and Apache Spark Streaming. These frameworks support parallel processing across multiple nodes, allowing organizations to scale their real-time processing infrastructure as needed.

2. Latency Reduction

Reducing processing latency is critical for real-time data processing applications, as delays in data ingestion and analysis can impact decision-making and responsiveness. To minimize latency, organizations can leverage in-memory computing technologies such as Apache Kafka and Apache Spark Streaming to process data in memory, reducing disk I/O and processing overhead. Additionally, optimizing data processing pipelines and using lightweight serialization formats such as Apache Avro can further reduce latency and improve overall system performance.

3. Data Quality Assurance

Maintaining data quality is essential for real-time data processing systems to ensure the accuracy and reliability of insights derived from streaming data. However, real-time data streams often contain noisy, incomplete, or inconsistent data, posing challenges for data quality assurance. To address these challenges, organizations can implement data validation and cleansing techniques within their data processing pipelines. Tools such as Apache Nifi and StreamSets Data Collector offer features for data quality monitoring, cleansing, and enrichment, enabling organizations to identify and correct data quality issues in real time.

4. Fault Tolerance

Real-time data processing systems must be resilient to failures to ensure uninterrupted operation and data consistency. Failures can occur at various levels of the data processing pipeline, including data ingestion, processing, and storage. To achieve fault tolerance, organizations can implement techniques such as data replication, checkpointing, and distributed consensus algorithms. Apache Kafka provides built-in support for replication and fault tolerance through its distributed architecture and fault-tolerant design. Additionally, Apache Flink and Apache Spark Streaming offer mechanisms for fault tolerance and state recovery, ensuring reliable and resilient data processing.

5. Complex Event Processing

Real-time data processing often involves analyzing complex event streams to detect patterns, correlations, and anomalies in the data. However, processing complex event streams in real time poses challenges in terms of event correlation, windowing, and aggregation. To address these challenges, organizations can leverage complex event processing (CEP) engines such as Apache Storm and Esper. These engines provide capabilities for event pattern matching, temporal windowing, and continuous query processing, enabling organizations to extract meaningful insights from complex event streams in real time.

6. Resource Management

Effective resource management is essential for optimizing the performance and efficiency of real-time data processing systems. Organizations must allocate resources judiciously to ensure that processing tasks are executed efficiently without overloading the system. To achieve optimal resource utilization, organizations can leverage resource management frameworks such as Apache YARN and Kubernetes. These frameworks provide features for dynamic resource allocation, scheduling, and isolation, enabling organizations to allocate resources based on workload demands and priorities.

Real-time data processing presents numerous challenges, including scalability, latency, data quality, fault tolerance, complex event processing, and resource management. However, by adopting the right technologies, techniques, and best practices, organizations can overcome these challenges and build robust, scalable, and resilient real-time data processing systems. From leveraging distributed data processing frameworks and in-memory computing technologies to implementing data validation and cleansing techniques, organizations can address the unique challenges of real-time data processing and unlock the full potential of streaming data for actionable insights and decision-making.

Implementing streaming analytics is crucial for organizations seeking to extract valuable insights from real-time data streams. Streaming analytics enables continuous monitoring, analysis, and response to dynamic data sources, allowing organizations to make informed decisions and take timely actions. Next, we will explore the fundamentals of implementing streaming analytics, including the architecture, key components, deployment techniques, and best practices.

1. Understanding Streaming Analytics Architecture

Streaming analytics architecture typically consists of three main components: data ingestion, processing, and visualization. Data is ingested from various sources such as sensors, logs, and social media feeds using streaming data ingestion frameworks like Apache Kafka or Amazon Kinesis. The ingested data is then processed in real time using stream processing engines like Apache Flink or Apache Spark Streaming. Finally, the processed insights are visualized and presented to end-users through dashboards or reporting tools.

2. Deploying Streaming Data Ingestion

To deploy a streaming data ingestion pipeline, organizations can leverage Apache Kafka, a distributed streaming platform known for its scalability and fault tolerance. To install Kafka, users can download the Kafka binaries from the Apache Kafka website and extract them to a desired location. They can then start the Kafka server using the following command:

bashCopy code

```
bin/kafka-server-start.sh config/server.properties
```

Once the Kafka server is up and running, users can create topics and start producing and consuming messages using the Kafka command-line tools.

3. Implementing Real-Time Processing with Apache Flink

Apache Flink is a powerful stream processing engine that supports event-time processing, stateful computations, and exactly-once semantics. To deploy a streaming analytics application with Flink, users can create a Flink project using Apache Maven or Gradle and add the Flink dependencies to their project's build file. They can then write streaming processing logic using Flink's DataStream API and submit the application to a Flink cluster for execution.

4. Visualizing Insights with Apache Superset

Apache Superset is an open-source data visualization platform that allows users to create interactive dashboards and visualizations from streaming data sources. To deploy Apache Superset, users can install Superset using Docker or deploy it to a cloud-based platform like AWS or Google Cloud Platform. Once deployed, users can connect Superset to their streaming data sources and create real-time dashboards to monitor key metrics and KPIs.

5. Best Practices for Streaming Analytics

Choose the Right Technologies: Select streaming data ingestion and processing technologies that align with your organization's requirements in terms of scalability, performance, and fault tolerance.

Optimize Resource Utilization: Ensure that your streaming analytics infrastructure is properly configured and optimized to handle the expected data volumes and processing workloads efficiently.

Monitor Performance and Latency: Implement monitoring and alerting mechanisms to track the performance and latency of your streaming analytics pipelines and identify potential bottlenecks or issues.

Ensure Data Quality: Implement data validation and cleansing techniques to ensure the accuracy and reliability of insights derived from streaming data sources.

Implement Disaster Recovery and Backup: Implement disaster recovery and backup strategies to protect against data loss and ensure business continuity in the event of failures or outages.

Implementing streaming analytics is essential for organizations looking to gain actionable insights from real-time data streams. By understanding the architecture, deploying the right technologies, and following best practices, organizations can build robust and scalable streaming analytics pipelines to monitor, analyze, and respond to dynamic data sources effectively. From deploying streaming data ingestion pipelines with Apache Kafka to processing real-time data with Apache Flink and visualizing insights with Apache Superset, organizations can leverage streaming analytics to drive data-driven decision-making and gain a competitive edge in today's fast-paced digital landscape.

Chapter 7: Integration of Unstructured Data in Big Data Warehousing

Handling unstructured data in data warehousing is a crucial aspect of modern data management strategies. As organizations continue to accumulate vast amounts of unstructured data from sources such as text documents, images, videos, and social media feeds, the ability to effectively store, process, and analyze this data alongside structured data is essential for gaining valuable insights and making informed decisions. Next, we will explore various techniques and best practices for handling unstructured data in data warehousing environments.

1. Understanding Unstructured Data

Unstructured data refers to data that does not have a predefined data model or organization. Unlike structured data, which is typically stored in databases with a well-defined schema, unstructured data comes in various formats and lacks a fixed structure. Examples of unstructured data include text documents, email messages, multimedia files, social media posts, and sensor data. Due to its diverse nature, unstructured data presents unique challenges for data warehousing and analysis.

2. Storing Unstructured Data

When storing unstructured data in a data warehousing environment, organizations have several options. One approach is to use a NoSQL database, such as MongoDB or Apache Cassandra, which is designed to handle unstructured and semi-structured data efficiently. NoSQL databases offer flexible schemas, horizontal scalability, and support for unstructured data types, making them well-suited for storing and managing diverse data types.

To deploy a NoSQL database like MongoDB, users can download the MongoDB Community Edition from the official website and follow the installation instructions for their operating system. Once installed, they can start the MongoDB server using the following command:

Copy code

mongod

3. Extracting Insights from Unstructured Data

Extracting meaningful insights from unstructured data requires specialized techniques for text mining, natural language processing (NLP), image analysis, and sentiment analysis. Text mining techniques, such as tokenization, stemming, and entity recognition, can help extract key information from textual documents. NLP algorithms, such as named entity recognition (NER) and sentiment analysis, can analyze text data to identify entities, sentiments, and topics.

To perform text mining and NLP tasks, organizations can leverage open-source libraries like NLTK (Natural Language Toolkit) and spaCy in Python. These libraries provide pre-trained models and algorithms for various NLP tasks, allowing users to analyze and extract insights from unstructured text data effectively.

4. Processing Multimedia Data

In addition to textual data, data warehousing systems may also need to handle multimedia data, such as images, videos, and audio files. Processing multimedia data often involves feature extraction, object detection, and image classification techniques. Convolutional neural networks (CNNs) and deep learning models, such as TensorFlow and PyTorch, are commonly used for analyzing and processing multimedia data.

To deploy a deep learning model for image classification using TensorFlow, users can install TensorFlow using

Python's package manager pip and then train a CNN model using labeled image datasets. Once trained, the model can be deployed to classify images and extract insights from multimedia data.

5. Integrating Unstructured Data with Structured Data

One of the key challenges in handling unstructured data is integrating it with structured data for comprehensive analysis. Data integration techniques, such as data fusion, entity resolution, and schema matching, can help reconcile differences between structured and unstructured data sources and create a unified view of the data.

To integrate unstructured data with structured data, organizations can use data integration tools and platforms that support both structured and unstructured data sources. These tools often provide connectors and adapters for various data formats and allow users to define mappings and transformations to harmonize the data.

6. Best Practices for Handling Unstructured Data

Understand the Data: Before processing unstructured data, it's essential to understand the nature and characteristics of the data to determine the appropriate processing techniques and algorithms.

Use Specialized Tools: Leverage specialized tools and libraries for text mining, NLP, image analysis, and multimedia processing to extract insights from unstructured data effectively.

Ensure Data Quality: Implement data quality checks and validation processes to ensure the accuracy, completeness, and consistency of unstructured data.

Scale with Distributed Computing: For large-scale processing of unstructured data, consider using distributed computing frameworks like Apache Hadoop and Apache Spark to distribute processing tasks across multiple nodes.

Monitor Performance: Monitor the performance of unstructured data processing pipelines to identify bottlenecks and optimize resource utilization for efficient processing.

Handling unstructured data in data warehousing environments is essential for organizations looking to leverage the full potential of their data assets. By understanding the characteristics of unstructured data, deploying appropriate storage and processing techniques, integrating unstructured data with structured data, and following best practices for data quality and performance optimization, organizations can unlock valuable insights and drive data-driven decision-making initiatives effectively.

Integrating unstructured data sources into data warehousing environments is a critical step in harnessing the full potential of data for analytics and decision-making. Unstructured data, such as text documents, images, videos, and social media feeds, often contains valuable insights that, when combined with structured data, can provide a comprehensive view of business operations and customer behavior. Next, we will explore various techniques for integrating unstructured data sources into data warehousing environments.

1. Data Ingestion

Data ingestion is the process of collecting and importing data from various sources into a data warehousing system. When dealing with unstructured data sources, such as text documents and multimedia files, data ingestion techniques may vary depending on the nature and format of the data.

For text documents, organizations can use data ingestion tools or custom scripts to extract text content from files and load it into the data warehouse. This process may involve parsing different file formats, such as PDF, Word documents, and plain text files, and extracting relevant information using text processing techniques.

To ingest multimedia data, organizations can leverage specialized tools or APIs provided by cloud storage platforms like Amazon S3 or Google Cloud Storage. These platforms often offer APIs for uploading and managing multimedia files, which can then be processed and analyzed using cloud-based services or on-premises infrastructure.

2. Data Extraction

Data extraction involves retrieving structured and unstructured data from its source systems and preparing it for loading into the data warehouse. For unstructured data sources, data extraction techniques may involve text mining, natural language processing (NLP), and image analysis to extract relevant information from text documents, social media feeds, and multimedia files.

Text mining techniques, such as tokenization, named entity recognition (NER), and sentiment analysis, can be used to extract key entities, sentiments, and topics from unstructured text data. NLP libraries like NLTK (Natural Language Toolkit) and spaCy provide pre-trained models and algorithms for performing these tasks efficiently.

For multimedia data, data extraction techniques may involve feature extraction, object detection, and image classification using deep learning models and frameworks like TensorFlow and PyTorch. These models can analyze images and videos to identify objects, scenes, and patterns relevant to the business context.

3. Data Transformation

Data transformation is the process of converting raw data into a format suitable for analysis and storage in the data warehouse. When integrating unstructured data sources, data transformation techniques may include converting text data into structured formats, extracting metadata from multimedia files, and normalizing data for consistency and compatibility with the data warehouse schema.

Text data extracted from documents and social media feeds can be transformed into structured formats, such as JSON or XML, using data transformation tools or custom scripts. Metadata extracted from multimedia files, such as image captions and timestamps, can be converted into structured attributes and stored alongside the raw data in the data warehouse.

4. Data Enrichment

Data enrichment involves enhancing raw data with additional information from external sources to provide more context and insights for analysis. When integrating unstructured data sources, data enrichment techniques may involve linking text documents to relevant entities in a knowledge graph, extracting geospatial information from multimedia files, and enriching social media data with user demographics and sentiment scores.

For example, text documents can be linked to relevant entities in a knowledge graph, such as people, organizations, and events, to provide additional context and insights. Multimedia files containing geospatial information, such as photos with location tags, can be enriched with latitude and longitude coordinates for spatial analysis.

5. Data Integration

Data integration is the process of combining data from different sources into a unified view for analysis and reporting. When integrating unstructured data sources, data integration techniques may involve merging structured and unstructured data sets, resolving inconsistencies and conflicts, and creating a unified data model for analysis.

Structured and unstructured data sets can be integrated using data integration tools and platforms that support both types of data sources. These tools often provide connectors and adapters for various data formats and allow users to define mappings and transformations to harmonize the data.

6. Data Quality Assurance

Data quality assurance involves ensuring the accuracy, completeness, and consistency of data throughout the integration process. When dealing with unstructured data sources, data quality assurance techniques may include validating text content for relevance and accuracy, verifying metadata consistency across multimedia files, and detecting anomalies and outliers in social media data.

To ensure data quality, organizations can implement data validation rules and checks at various stages of the integration process, such as data ingestion, extraction, transformation, and loading. Automated data quality tools and algorithms can help identify and address data quality issues in real time, ensuring that only high-quality data is stored in the data warehouse.

Integrating unstructured data sources into data warehousing environments requires careful planning, specialized tools, and expertise in text mining, NLP, image analysis, and multimedia processing. By leveraging data ingestion, extraction, transformation, enrichment, integration, and quality assurance techniques, organizations can unlock valuable insights from unstructured data and make informed decisions to drive business success.

Chapter 8: Data Governance and Security in Big Data Analytics

Governance frameworks for big data are essential structures that provide guidelines, policies, and procedures for managing and ensuring the quality, security, privacy, and compliance of data within big data environments. These frameworks help organizations establish accountability, transparency, and trust in their data assets, enabling them to maximize the value of their data while mitigating risks and ensuring regulatory compliance. Next, we will explore various governance frameworks for big data and their importance in modern data-driven organizations.

1. Introduction to Governance Frameworks

Governance frameworks provide a structured approach to managing data across the entire data lifecycle, from data acquisition and ingestion to storage, processing, analysis, and dissemination. They encompass various aspects of data governance, including data management, data quality, data security, data privacy, and regulatory compliance.

2. Components of Governance Frameworks

Governance frameworks typically consist of several key components, including:

Policies and procedures: These documents define the rules, standards, and guidelines for data management, security, privacy, and compliance.

Roles and responsibilities: Governance frameworks assign specific roles and responsibilities to individuals or teams responsible for implementing and enforcing governance policies.

Data stewardship: Data stewardship involves the management and oversight of data assets to ensure their integrity, quality, and usability.

Data lifecycle management: Governance frameworks define processes and workflows for managing data throughout its lifecycle, from creation and acquisition to archiving and disposal.

Risk management: Governance frameworks include mechanisms for identifying, assessing, and mitigating risks associated with data management, security, and privacy.

Compliance management: Governance frameworks ensure that organizations comply with relevant laws, regulations, and industry standards governing data privacy, security, and disclosure.

3. Importance of Governance Frameworks

Governance frameworks are essential for ensuring the effective and responsible use of big data in organizations. They provide several key benefits, including:

Risk mitigation: Governance frameworks help organizations identify and mitigate risks associated with data management, security breaches, and regulatory non-compliance.

Data quality assurance: Governance frameworks establish standards and processes for ensuring the accuracy, completeness, and consistency of data, improving the quality and reliability of decision-making.

Regulatory compliance: Governance frameworks ensure that organizations comply with applicable laws, regulations, and industry standards governing data privacy, security, and disclosure.

Stakeholder trust: Governance frameworks promote transparency, accountability, and trust in data management practices, enhancing stakeholder confidence in the organization's data assets.

Operational efficiency: Governance frameworks streamline data management processes, reducing complexity, duplication, and inefficiencies in data workflows.

Data-driven decision-making: Governance frameworks enable organizations to leverage data effectively for decision-making, innovation, and competitive advantage.

4. Implementing Governance Frameworks

Implementing governance frameworks requires a coordinated effort involving multiple stakeholders, including executives, data stewards, IT professionals, and legal and compliance experts. The following steps can help organizations effectively implement governance frameworks for big data:

Assess current state: Evaluate existing data management practices, policies, and technologies to identify strengths, weaknesses, and areas for improvement.

Define governance objectives: Clearly define the goals and objectives of the governance framework, aligning them with organizational priorities, strategic initiatives, and regulatory requirements.

Develop governance policies: Develop comprehensive policies and procedures for data management, security, privacy, and compliance, ensuring alignment with industry best practices and regulatory standards.

Establish governance structures: Define roles, responsibilities, and reporting relationships for individuals and teams responsible for implementing and enforcing governance policies.

Implement governance technologies: Deploy appropriate technologies, tools, and platforms to support governance objectives, including data governance software, metadata management tools, and security and privacy solutions.

Monitor and enforce compliance: Regularly monitor data management activities, assess compliance with governance policies, and take corrective actions as needed to address non-compliance issues.

Continuously improve: Continuously review and update the governance framework to adapt to changing business needs, technological advancements, and regulatory requirements.

5. Case Studies and Best Practices

Case studies and best practices provide valuable insights into successful governance implementations and lessons learned from real-world experiences. Organizations can learn from the experiences of others and apply best practices to their own governance initiatives.

Governance frameworks are essential for managing and ensuring the quality, security, privacy, and compliance of big data in organizations. By establishing clear policies, roles, processes, and technologies for data governance, organizations can maximize the value of their data assets while mitigating risks and ensuring regulatory compliance.

Security considerations in big data analytics environments are of paramount importance due to the massive volumes of sensitive data processed and stored in these systems. As organizations increasingly rely on big data analytics to derive insights and make data-driven decisions, they must prioritize the implementation of robust security measures to protect against various threats, including data breaches, unauthorized access, and cyberattacks. Next, we will explore the key security considerations and best practices for securing big data analytics environments.

1. Introduction to Security in Big Data Analytics

Security in big data analytics encompasses a wide range of measures aimed at protecting data confidentiality, integrity, and availability throughout the data lifecycle. It involves implementing safeguards to prevent unauthorized access, data theft, and other security incidents that could compromise the confidentiality, integrity, or availability of sensitive information.

2. Threat Landscape

Big data analytics environments face a diverse range of security threats, including:

Data breaches: Unauthorized access to sensitive data, resulting in data theft or exposure.

Insider threats: Malicious or negligent actions by internal users, employees, or contractors.

Malware and ransomware: Malicious software designed to disrupt operations, steal data, or extort money.

Distributed denial of service (DDoS) attacks: Coordinated attacks aimed at overwhelming systems with a flood of traffic, leading to service disruptions.

Advanced persistent threats (APTs): Sophisticated, targeted attacks that persistently target specific organizations or individuals over an extended period.

3. Security Considerations

To mitigate security risks in big data analytics environments, organizations should consider the following security measures:

Access control: Implement strong access controls to restrict access to sensitive data and systems based on user roles, permissions, and privileges.

Encryption: Encrypt data at rest and in transit to protect it from unauthorized access, interception, and tampering.

Authentication: Use multi-factor authentication (MFA) and strong authentication mechanisms to verify the identity of users and prevent unauthorized access.

Data masking and anonymization: Mask or anonymize sensitive data to protect individual privacy and comply with data protection regulations.

Auditing and logging: Implement auditing and logging mechanisms to track and monitor user activities, system events, and data access for compliance and security purposes.

Security monitoring: Deploy intrusion detection and prevention systems (IDPS) and security information and event management (SIEM) solutions to monitor and detect security threats and incidents in real time.

Incident response: Develop and implement incident response plans and procedures to effectively respond to and mitigate security incidents, breaches, and data breaches.

Security awareness training: Provide security awareness training and education to employees, users, and stakeholders to raise awareness of security risks and best practices.

4. Best Practices

To enhance security in big data analytics environments, organizations should adhere to the following best practices:

Implement a defense-in-depth approach: Use multiple layers of security controls, including network security, endpoint security, and data security, to protect against various security threats.

Regularly update and patch systems: Keep systems, applications, and software up to date with the latest security patches and updates to address known vulnerabilities and security flaws.

Conduct security assessments and audits: Regularly assess and audit the security posture of big data analytics environments to identify and remediate security gaps and weaknesses.

Collaborate with security partners: Work closely with security vendors, partners, and industry peers to share threat intelligence, best practices, and security insights.

Stay informed about emerging threats: Keep abreast of the latest security threats, trends, and best practices in the cybersecurity landscape to proactively identify and mitigate security risks.

5. Case Studies

Case studies provide valuable insights into real-world security incidents, breaches, and best practices for securing big data analytics environments. Organizations can learn from the experiences of others and apply lessons learned to enhance their own security posture.

Security considerations are critical in big data analytics environments to protect against various security threats and risks. By implementing robust security measures, organizations can safeguard sensitive data, mitigate security risks, and ensure the confidentiality, integrity, and availability of their data assets in the face of evolving cybersecurity threats.

Chapter 9: Optimizing Big Data Performance and Resource Management

Performance optimization is a critical aspect of big data analytics, ensuring that organizations can derive insights quickly and efficiently from large and complex datasets. Next, we will explore various strategies and techniques for optimizing the performance of big data analytics systems, including data processing engines, storage solutions, and query execution.

1. Introduction to Performance Optimization

Performance optimization in big data analytics involves enhancing the speed, scalability, and efficiency of data processing and analysis tasks. By optimizing performance, organizations can reduce processing times, improve resource utilization, and enhance overall productivity in handling large volumes of data.

2. Scalable Data Storage Solutions

One key aspect of performance optimization is selecting and deploying scalable data storage solutions that can efficiently handle the storage and retrieval of large datasets. Technologies such as distributed file systems (e.g., Hadoop Distributed File System, Amazon S3) and NoSQL databases (e.g., Apache Cassandra, MongoDB) provide scalability and fault tolerance, allowing organizations to store and access massive volumes of data across distributed clusters.

3. Data Partitioning and Sharding

Partitioning and sharding are techniques used to distribute data across multiple nodes or partitions to improve performance and scalability. By partitioning data based on certain criteria (e.g., date, geographical location, customer ID), organizations can distribute data processing tasks across multiple nodes in parallel, reducing processing times and improving overall performance.

4. Parallel Processing and Distributed Computing

Parallel processing and distributed computing are fundamental principles in big data analytics for achieving high performance and scalability. Technologies such as Apache Hadoop and Apache Spark leverage parallel processing techniques to distribute data processing tasks across multiple nodes in a cluster, enabling faster execution of data-intensive computations and analytics.

5. In-Memory Computing

In-memory computing involves storing and processing data in memory rather than on disk, resulting in significantly faster data access and processing times. Technologies such as Apache Ignite and Apache Flink leverage in-memory computing to achieve real-time processing and analytics on large datasets, enabling organizations to derive insights faster and more efficiently.

6. Query Optimization Techniques

Query optimization is crucial for improving the performance of analytical queries and data retrieval operations. Techniques such as query rewriting, indexing, and query caching can significantly reduce query execution times and improve overall system performance. Additionally, organizations can leverage query optimization tools and frameworks (e.g., Apache Calcite, Presto) to automatically optimize and tune queries for better performance.

7. Data Compression and Encoding

Data compression and encoding techniques can help reduce storage requirements and improve data transfer speeds in big data analytics environments. By compressing data before storage and transmission, organizations can save storage space and reduce network bandwidth usage, resulting in faster data processing and analysis.

8. Resource Management and Optimization

Effective resource management is essential for optimizing the performance of big data analytics systems. Technologies such as Apache YARN and Kubernetes enable organizations to dynamically allocate and manage compute, memory, and storage resources based on workload requirements, ensuring optimal resource utilization and performance.

9. Caching and Memoization

Caching and memoization are techniques used to store and reuse intermediate results and computations to avoid redundant calculations and improve performance. By caching frequently accessed data and computation results in memory or on disk, organizations can reduce computation times and improve overall system responsiveness.

10. Monitoring and Performance Tuning

Continuous monitoring and performance tuning are essential for maintaining optimal performance in big data analytics environments. Organizations should regularly monitor system performance metrics (e.g., CPU utilization, memory usage, disk I/O) and identify performance bottlenecks and optimization opportunities. Additionally, performance tuning activities such as query profiling, index optimization, and resource allocation adjustments can help improve system performance over time.

Performance optimization is a critical aspect of big data analytics, enabling organizations to derive insights quickly and efficiently from large and complex datasets. By implementing scalable storage solutions, parallel processing techniques, query optimization strategies, and effective resource management practices, organizations can optimize the performance of their big data analytics systems and drive greater value from their data assets.

Efficient resource management is crucial in any computing environment, especially in the context of big data analytics where large volumes of data and complex processing tasks require significant computational resources. Next, we will explore various techniques and strategies for efficient resource management in big data analytics environments, including workload scheduling, resource allocation, containerization, and auto-scaling.

1. Workload Scheduling

Workload scheduling involves distributing data processing tasks and analytical jobs across computing resources in a way that maximizes resource utilization and minimizes job completion times. Technologies such as Apache Hadoop YARN and Kubernetes provide robust workload scheduling capabilities, allowing organizations to schedule and manage jobs across distributed clusters efficiently.

2. Resource Allocation

Resource allocation is the process of assigning compute, memory, and storage resources to different tasks and applications based on their requirements and priorities. By dynamically allocating resources based on workload demands, organizations can optimize resource utilization and ensure that critical tasks receive the necessary resources to meet their performance objectives.

3. Containerization

Containerization technologies such as Docker and Kubernetes have gained popularity in big data analytics environments for their ability to package applications and dependencies into lightweight, portable containers. By containerizing applications and services, organizations can isolate workloads, improve resource utilization, and streamline deployment and management processes.

4. Virtualization

Virtualization technologies such as VMware and Xen enable organizations to abstract physical hardware resources and create virtual machines (VMs) with isolated computing environments. By virtualizing resources, organizations can achieve better resource utilization, scalability, and flexibility in managing compute, memory, and storage resources across distributed clusters.

5. Auto-Scaling

Auto-scaling is a dynamic resource management technique that automatically adjusts computing resources based on workload demands. Cloud computing platforms such as Amazon Web Services (AWS) and Microsoft Azure provide auto-scaling capabilities that allow organizations to scale compute instances up or down in response to changes in workload demand, ensuring optimal resource utilization and performance.

6. Resource Quotas and Limits

Resource quotas and limits enable organizations to enforce resource usage policies and prevent individual tasks or applications from consuming excessive resources. By setting resource quotas and limits, organizations can ensure fair resource allocation, prevent resource contention, and avoid performance degradation due to overutilization of resources.

7. Resource Monitoring and Optimization

Continuous monitoring of resource usage metrics such as CPU utilization, memory usage, and disk I/O is essential for identifying performance bottlenecks and optimizing resource allocation. By analyzing resource usage patterns and trends, organizations can identify opportunities for optimization and fine-tune resource allocation to improve overall system performance.

8. Cost Optimization

Cost optimization is an important aspect of resource management, especially in cloud computing environments where resource usage directly impacts operational expenses. By optimizing resource utilization, organizations can minimize infrastructure costs, improve cost-efficiency, and maximize return on investment (ROI) in their big data analytics initiatives.

9. Policy-based Resource Management

Policy-based resource management involves defining and enforcing policies for resource allocation, utilization, and optimization based on organizational requirements and priorities. By implementing policy-based resource management strategies, organizations can ensure compliance with resource usage guidelines, improve operational efficiency, and maintain service level agreements (SLAs) for critical applications and workloads.

10. Dynamic Resource Provisioning

Dynamic resource provisioning techniques such as elastic scaling and on-demand resource allocation enable organizations to dynamically adjust resource allocation based on real-time workload demands. By provisioning resources dynamically, organizations can adapt to changing workload patterns, optimize resource utilization, and ensure optimal performance and scalability in big data analytics environments.

Efficient resource management is essential for maximizing the performance, scalability, and cost-effectiveness of big data analytics environments. By implementing workload scheduling, resource allocation, containerization, auto-scaling, and other resource management techniques, organizations can optimize resource utilization, improve operational efficiency, and achieve better outcomes from their big data analytics initiatives.

Chapter 10: Case Studies and Best Practices in Big Data Analytics Integration

Real-world case studies provide valuable insights into the challenges, solutions, and best practices involved in integrating big data analytics into various industries and domains. Next, we will examine several case studies of successful big data analytics integration, highlighting key strategies, technologies, and outcomes.

1. Retail Industry

In the retail industry, big data analytics integration has revolutionized customer segmentation, personalized marketing, and supply chain optimization. One notable case study is Walmart's use of big data analytics to optimize inventory management and enhance the customer shopping experience. By analyzing sales data, customer demographics, and social media interactions, Walmart can predict demand patterns, optimize product placement, and tailor promotions to individual customer preferences. The use of data analytics has enabled Walmart to increase sales, reduce costs, and improve customer satisfaction.

2. Healthcare Sector

In the healthcare sector, big data analytics integration has transformed patient care, disease management, and medical research. An example is the Mayo Clinic's use of big data analytics to improve patient outcomes and operational efficiency. By analyzing electronic health records (EHRs), medical imaging data, and genomic data, the Mayo Clinic can identify trends, patterns, and risk factors for various diseases, personalize treatment plans, and optimize healthcare delivery. The use of data analytics has enabled the Mayo Clinic to enhance patient care, reduce hospital readmissions, and advance medical research.

3. Financial Services

In the financial services industry, big data analytics integration has revolutionized risk management, fraud detection, and customer insights. A prominent case study is Capital One's use of big data analytics to enhance credit risk assessment and fraud detection. By analyzing transaction data, credit card usage patterns, and customer behavior, Capital One can identify potential risks, detect fraudulent activities, and personalize financial products and services. The use of data analytics has enabled Capital One to mitigate risks, reduce fraud losses, and improve customer satisfaction.

4. Manufacturing Sector

In the manufacturing sector, big data analytics integration has optimized production processes, supply chain management, and predictive maintenance. A notable case study is General Electric's use of big data analytics to optimize industrial operations and equipment maintenance. By analyzing sensor data, machine performance metrics, and historical maintenance records, General Electric can predict equipment failures, schedule maintenance tasks proactively, and optimize production schedules. The use of data analytics has enabled General Electric to increase equipment uptime, reduce maintenance costs, and improve operational efficiency.

5. Transportation Industry

In the transportation industry, big data analytics integration has revolutionized logistics management, route optimization, and fleet maintenance. An example is UPS's use of big data analytics to optimize delivery routes and reduce fuel consumption. By analyzing traffic patterns, weather conditions, and package delivery data, UPS can optimize delivery routes, minimize fuel consumption, and reduce carbon emissions. The use of data analytics has enabled UPS to improve operational efficiency, reduce costs, and enhance environmental sustainability.

6. Telecommunications Sector

In the telecommunications sector, big data analytics integration has transformed network optimization, customer experience management, and marketing analytics. A notable case study is AT&T's use of big data analytics to improve network performance and customer satisfaction. By analyzing network traffic data, customer usage patterns, and quality of service metrics, AT&T can identify network bottlenecks, optimize network capacity, and personalize customer interactions. The use of data analytics has enabled AT&T to enhance network reliability, reduce churn rates, and drive revenue growth.

These case studies highlight the diverse applications and benefits of big data analytics integration across various industries and domains. By leveraging advanced analytics techniques and technologies, organizations can unlock valuable insights from their data, drive innovation, and gain a competitive edge in today's data-driven economy.

Effective integration of big data analytics involves various practices and strategies aimed at maximizing the value of data assets and driving actionable insights. Next, we will explore best practices for successful big data analytics integration, covering key principles, methodologies, and technologies.

1. Define Clear Business Objectives

Before embarking on a big data analytics integration initiative, it's crucial to define clear business objectives and align them with organizational goals. This involves understanding the specific challenges, opportunities, and use cases that big data analytics can address. For example, a retail organization may aim to improve customer segmentation, personalized marketing, and inventory optimization. By defining clear business objectives, organizations can prioritize initiatives, allocate resources effectively, and measure the success of their analytics projects.

2. Establish Robust Data Governance Framework

A robust data governance framework is essential for ensuring the quality, security, and compliance of data used in big data analytics integration. This involves defining data ownership, roles, and responsibilities, establishing data quality standards, and implementing security controls. Organizations should also ensure compliance with regulations such as GDPR, HIPAA, and CCPA to protect sensitive data and maintain trust with customers. Tools like Apache Ranger and Apache Atlas can help enforce data governance policies and manage metadata effectively.

3. Adopt Agile Methodologies

Agile methodologies promote iterative development, collaboration, and flexibility, making them well-suited for big data analytics integration projects. By breaking down complex tasks into smaller, manageable units called sprints, organizations can deliver value incrementally and adapt to changing requirements. Agile practices such as daily stand-up meetings, sprint planning, and retrospectives facilitate communication and alignment across teams, ensuring that analytics initiatives remain on track and deliver tangible outcomes.

4. Leverage Scalable Infrastructure

Scalable infrastructure is essential for supporting the storage, processing, and analysis of large volumes of data in a cost-effective manner. Cloud platforms like Amazon Web

Services (AWS), Microsoft Azure, and Google Cloud Platform (GCP) offer scalable storage solutions such as Amazon S3, Azure Blob Storage, and Google Cloud Storage, as well as managed big data services like Amazon EMR, Azure HDInsight, and Google Dataproc. These platforms enable organizations to scale resources up or down based on demand, ensuring optimal performance and cost efficiency.

5. Embrace Data Integration Technologies

Data integration technologies play a crucial role in consolidating data from disparate sources, transforming it into actionable insights, and delivering it to end-users. Tools like Apache Kafka, Apache NiFi, and Talend facilitate real-time data ingestion, processing, and integration across heterogeneous environments. These platforms support a wide range of data formats, protocols, and connectors, enabling organizations to ingest data from sources such as databases, streaming platforms, IoT devices, and APIs.

6. Implement Data Quality Assurance

Data quality assurance is essential for ensuring the accuracy, completeness, and consistency of data used in big data analytics integration. This involves performing data profiling, cleansing, deduplication, and validation to identify and correct errors, anomalies, and inconsistencies. Tools like Apache Spark, Trifacta, and Informatica offer data quality features and functionalities to automate these tasks and improve the reliability of analytics insights.

7. Foster Data Literacy and Collaboration

Data literacy and collaboration are critical for empowering stakeholders to make informed decisions and derive value from big data analytics. Organizations should invest in training programs, workshops, and knowledge-sharing sessions to enhance the data literacy of employees across departments. Collaboration platforms like Slack, Microsoft Teams, and Confluence facilitate communication, knowledge sharing, and collaboration among data scientists, analysts, and business users, enabling them to work together effectively to derive insights and drive business outcomes.

8. Monitor and Measure Performance

Continuous monitoring and measurement of performance metrics are essential for evaluating the effectiveness of big data analytics integration initiatives and identifying areas for improvement. Key performance indicators (KPIs) such as data quality, processing speed, resource utilization, and user satisfaction can help organizations assess the impact of analytics projects on business outcomes. Tools like Apache Ambari, Grafana, and Splunk provide monitoring and analytics capabilities to track KPIs, detect anomalies, and optimize performance in real time.

By following these best practices for effective big data analytics integration, organizations can harness the power of data to drive innovation, gain competitive advantage, and deliver value to customers. By defining clear business objectives, establishing robust data governance, adopting agile methodologies, leveraging scalable infrastructure, embracing data integration technologies, implementing data quality assurance, fostering data literacy and collaboration, and monitoring performance, organizations can maximize the success of their analytics initiatives and achieve their strategic goals.

Conclusion

In summary, the "Data Warehousing: Optimizing Data Storage and Retrieval for Business Success" bundle offers a comprehensive exploration of the essential concepts, techniques, and strategies for building and leveraging data warehouses effectively. Across four insightful books, readers are taken on a journey from understanding the fundamentals of data warehousing to mastering advanced techniques and harnessing the power of big data analytics.

In "Book 1 - Data Warehousing Fundamentals: A Beginner's Guide," readers are provided with a solid foundation in data warehousing concepts, including the importance of data modeling, extraction, transformation, and loading (ETL) processes. This beginner-friendly guide equips readers with the knowledge needed to embark on their data warehousing journey with confidence.

"Book 2 - Mastering Data Modeling for Data Warehousing" delves deeper into the intricacies of data modeling, offering readers a comprehensive understanding of conceptual, logical, and dimensional modeling techniques. By mastering these modeling principles, readers can design efficient and scalable data warehouses that meet the evolving needs of their organizations.

"Book 3 - Advanced ETL Techniques for Data Warehousing Optimization" takes readers on a journey into the realm of advanced ETL techniques, exploring strategies for optimizing data extraction, transformation, and loading processes. From incremental loading to change data capture (CDC), readers learn how to streamline ETL workflows and improve the efficiency of their data warehousing operations.

Finally, "Book 4 - Big Data Analytics: Harnessing the Power of Data Warehousing for Experts" explores how organizations can leverage their data warehouses to unlock valuable insights and drive informed decision-making. From real-time data processing to predictive modeling, readers discover how to harness the power of big data analytics to gain a competitive edge in today's data-driven business landscape.

Collectively, these four books provide readers with a comprehensive toolkit for optimizing data storage and retrieval, empowering them to harness the full potential of their data assets and drive business success. Whether you're a beginner embarking on your data warehousing journey or an expert looking to sharpen your skills, this bundle has something to offer for everyone striving to unlock the transformative power of data.